CLASSIC
BOOK OF
RUDE JOKES

CLASSIC BOOK OF RUDE JOKES

CRASS HUMOR FOR THE DISCRIMINATING JOKESTER

BY SCOTT McNEELY

CHRONICLE BOOKS

San Francisco

Text copyright © 2013 by Scott McNeely.
All rights reserved. No part of this book may be reproduced in any form without written permission from the publisher.

Library of Congress Cataloging-in-Publication Data available.

ISBN: 978-1-4521-1698-3

Manufactured in China

Designed by Barbara Genetin

10 9 8 7 6 5 4 3 2 1

Chronicle Books LLC
680 Second Street
San Francisco, California 94107
www.chroniclebooks.com

MIX
Paper
FSC FSC® C016973

This volume of rude and offensive jokes is dedicated to my family, who remain anonymous by request.

("Honey, don't you dare put my name in that book.")

CONTENTS

INTRODUCTION 8

1: IT'S IMPORTANT TO LAUGH 10

2: RUDE "DIFFERENTLY ABLED" 26

3: RUDE BLONDES 44

4: RUDE RELIGION 56

5: RUDE RACISTS 76

6: RUDE RELATIONSHIPS 98

7: RUDE SEX 112

8: SICK & TWISTED 136

INTRODUCTION

WHY DID I WRITE THE *CLASSIC BOOK OF RUDE JOKES*? THAT'S A QUESTION MY WIFE HAS BEEN ASKING FOR MONTHS: WHY, INDEED, WOULD I DISGRACE MY FAMILY BY WRITING A BOOK FILLED WITH RUDE, OFFENSIVE, INSENSITIVE, MISOGYNISTIC, AND RACIST JOKES?

Before explaining why I wrote the book, some context is required. Most joke books I've read are emphatically *not* funny. And don't get me started on the pitiful state of humor on the Internet. There's nothing amusing about look-alike websites peddling carbon-copy lists of mediocre jokes.

So, a few years ago, I decided to write a book called the *Ultimate Book of Jokes*. I asked friends to send me their favorite one-liners; many graciously complied. I scoured secondhand bookshops and mercilessly harangued colleagues, friends' children, and random people on the street, always on the hunt for laugh-inducing source material.

The *Ultimate Book of Jokes* has been well received; but, interestingly, readers have had two conflicting criticisms. Many readers have demanded *fewer* kid jokes and *more* dirty and offensive jokes. At the same time, some readers have complained about too many curse words in a title intended for joke lovers of all ages.

Fast-forward a few years and—voilà!—problem solved. Meet the *Classic Book of Rude Jokes*, with only the most offensive and rude jokes included and featuring extra sections on misogyny, insensitivity, and racism. With 50 percent more swear words, too!

The *Classic Book of Rude Jokes* is intended, unapologetically, for people who enjoy a hearty laugh and who know how to take a joke.

It's been said that nobody ever tells a joke for the first time. I do not claim otherwise. Each joke in this book has been around the block a few times, because joke books are not written so much as they are curated. My job has been to sort the comedic wheat from the chaff, to polish language and sharpen punch lines, and to provide some cultural perspective.

—SCOTT MCNEELY

1

IT'S IMPORTANT TO LAUGH

THE SEVENTEENTH-CENTURY ENGLISH WRITER JOSEPH ADDISON ONCE SAID, "MAN IS DISTINGUISHED FROM ALL OTHER CREATURES BY THE FACULTY OF LAUGHTER." AND IT'S TRUE: WE HUMANS ARE NOTABLE FOR THE RANGE AND COMPLEXITY OF OUR HUMOR. WIT, SATIRE, SARCASM, IRONY, FARCE, SLAPSTICK—WE FIND MANY WAYS TO MAKE OURSELVES LAUGH.

Of course, this marvelous capacity to laugh is often paired with subject matter that would make a whore blush: farts, bawdy plays on the word *cock*, and ribaldry at the expense of alcoholics, men of the cloth, loose women, and midgets. Somehow we can make ourselves laugh at dead babies, blind people, Jews, Italians, Canadians, lawyers, and rednecks. No race or ethnicity is spared; no sexual orientation or hobby or character flaw escapes the spotlight. Jokes are the ultimate social equalizer.

Can jokes go too far? Can they hurt feelings? Absolutely. It's guaranteed that more than one joke in this book will offend you; it simply goes with the territory. Just remember that the events depicted in jokes are fictitious. Similarities to any persons living or dead are merely coincidental.

WHAT IS A JOKE?

What's the difference between a joke and a funny story? One of the big differences is the buildup to a punch line. Jokes have punch lines, funny stories usually don't.

Jokes are also mercifully short. Two or three lines is all you need for a joke to hit its target. And often jokes have a formulaic setup that hastens the climax (think: yo mama jokes, bar jokes, light-bulb jokes, knock-knock jokes, etc.).

After reading a few thousand jokes, it's also clear that jokes fall into two broad categories that humans—no doubt since the dawn of time—have found irresistibly funny. The first is so-called situational humor where an incongruous situation or a false assumption prompts a howl of laughter. The hallmarks of these jokes are talking animals, wish-granting genies, and foul-mouthed priests. Whenever day-to-day reality is even slightly distorted, it's a golden opportunity for an unexpected—and unexpectedly funny—punch line.

The second category involves wordplay. Double entendres and clever turns of phrase are the hallmarks here. Late-night television hosts and stand-up comedians are the masters of this style of humor. Think of Johnny Carson, David Letterman, Jon Stewart, and Monty Python's merry pranksters.

WHY WE LAUGH

Why do we laugh at jokes? Scientists and professors, theorists and folklorists, not to mention bartenders and late-night comedians, have all thought deeply about this question. No surprise, then, that there are many theories of laughter—how laughter relieves inhibition, how laughter allows us to metaphorically beat up our social superiors, how laughter gives us a mechanism for dealing with socially taboo subjects such as racism, homosexuality, infidelity, and death.

None other than Sigmund Freud argued that jokes, like dreams, are reflections of our unconscious desires and allow us publicly to share our sexual, aggressive, and cynical tendencies (which otherwise remain locked away in our subconscious).

Fair enough. But that doesn't satisfy the question of why we *laugh* instead of simply clap when somebody tells a rip-roaring joke. One theory argues that laughing itself promotes good health: Studies have shown that laughing lowers blood pressure, reduces stress hormones, and boosts your immune system. Laughter also triggers the release of endorphins, the body's natural painkillers, and produces a general sense of well-being.

Translation: People who laugh at jokes are likely to endure life's vicissitudes better than humorless sticks-in-the-mud who rarely crack a smile. Think of laughing as a mini-workout for your body, mind, and spirit.

AM I A SEXIST, RACIST HATER FOR LAUGHING?

The thing about jokes is that there's inevitably a target or victim. Every joke has a butt. And *nobody* likes being a butt. It's in the very nature of jokes to throw salt on the wounds of people caught in their comedic nets.

Are jokes hurtful? Yes.

Is it okay to laugh? Yes.

What's not okay is telling a joke with the explicit intent to hurt somebody's feelings. And the only way to understand intent is to understand context. Is it okay to tell a blow-job joke to your girlfriend's parents? Or a lawyer joke to a group of lawyers? What if Barack Obama told a Bill Clinton sex joke to Hillary? Or to Chelsea?

The very same joke can come across as hilariously funny, mean-spirited, harassing, or straight-up hateful. It all depends on how well you know your audience. And on how much your audience trusts your intentions.

"Guns don't kill people," the saying goes, "people kill people." It's a similar story with jokes.

As with so many things in life, the Golden Rule comes in handy: Joke unto others as you would have others joke unto you. Follow this simple advice and you'll always laugh with a clear conscience.

IT'S IMPORTANT TO LAUGH

THE JOKE'S ON YOU

In 2001, Professor Richard Wiseman decided to answer the question, What is the world's funniest joke? He created the LaughLab Project (www.laughlab.co.uk) to investigate this age-old riddle using modern scientific methods. After more than 40,000 joke submissions and more than 1.5 million ratings from joke lovers around the world, Professor Wiseman had his answer. Without further ado, the world's funniest joke according to LaughLab:

> *Two hunters are out in the woods when one of them collapses. He doesn't seem to be breathing and his eyes are glazed. The other guy whips out his phone and calls emergency services. He gasps, "My friend is dead! What can I do?"*
>
> *The operator says, "Calm down. I can help. First, let's make sure he's dead."*
>
> *There is a silence, then a shot is heard. Back on the phone, the guy says, "Okay, now what?"*

Unfortunately, it turns out the world's funniest joke is not very funny. It rates a chuckle, for sure. Yet is it the funniest joke on planet Earth? Not by a long shot.

The problem is that most of us are not hunters. The culture of hunting is not part of our daily experience (apologies to the avid hunters reading this book). So the premise, while obviously humorous, feels distant. We're hearing a story about random people with whom we share few direct connections. And this points to a deeper truth about jokes: The funny ones hit close to home. The funniest jokes leverage your own experiences, and often your own insecurities, to make a point.

For this reason there never can be a single "funniest" joke. What you find funny is always filtered through the prism of personal experience and cultural perspective.

CURSE WORDS: SAY THEM LOUD AND PROUD

Here's an interesting fact: In books from the fourteenth century you rarely encounter the words *damn* or *God*. Back then it was considered blasphemous to take the Lord's name in vain or to use epithets such as *damned*. When late medieval writers wanted to curse, they preferred nonblasphemous expressions such as *zounds* (which means "God's wounds"), *fie*, *bastard*, and *cuckold* (insulting one's parentage or rank in society, in ye olde days, was the very worst kind of affront).

Interestingly, those same medieval writers didn't think twice about using words like *cock*, *fuck*, and *cunt* (or *cunte* or *coynte* or one of a dozen medieval variations for representing the female genitalia in print). Which makes you wonder: What is it about words like *fuck*, *shit*, and *cunt* that makes them so vulgar today? Why are these garden-variety fourteenth-century words considered so goddamned offensive in the twenty-first century?

The funny thing is, nobody really knows. Linguists and psychologists have studied the question, and there is no agreement on why certain words are considered more offensive than others. Or why the same word—with the exact same meaning—is perceived as vulgar in one era and inoffensive in a different era.

Social scientists do agree that people swear to express their frustration, anger, or surprise. They also agree that swearing has benefits. Swearing can be cathartic—it allows our overwrought feelings an escape valve. Swear words boost office productivity (work environments with mild profanity and friendly insults apparently promote group unity). And swear words are frequently used to accent the positive: "You are fucking awesome!" is a much stronger compliment—and more quickly understood by others as such—than simply saying, "You are awesome!"

Social science also agrees that virtually all people swear, and swear consistently throughout their lifetimes. Research has shown that all people, no matter what country they live in, swear an average of 0.7 percent of the time (compared to a 1 percent rate for common words such as *I* and *you* appearing in speech).

And when we do swear, we chose our words carefully (if often subconsciously), depending on the social setting. Studies have

Top Five Lame Swear Words

Call them substitute curse words, minced oaths, or simply "nice" swear words–these five mild turns of phrase are never okay to use. Ever.

SHAZBOT: A gentle curse word from the late 1970s television show *Mork and Mindy*. Go fork yourself, Robin Williams.

FRAK: The nice way to say fuck, courtesy of the new and improved *Battlestar Galactica* television show. "Frak you! Frak off! You've got to be frakking kidding me!"

SCHEISSE: The German word for "shit" is typically uttered by annoying people who think it's less offensive to curse in a foreign language. (We *merde* on your false assumptions.)

GOSH DARN: C'mon people, taking the name of Gosh in vain leads you straight to Heck.

BLEEP: As in, "This bleeping movie sucks!" It's often said the censorship is the height of vanity. If so, then self-censoring bleeps are like making love to yourself in your own mouth (or something like that). Reach for "fudge" or "shoot" or "yikes" before reaching for the indecorous "bleep."

Top Twenty-Eight Rude and Offensive Words

Why are some words more offensive than others? Some linguists believe that highly offensive curse words share similar structures: the presence of fricatives (the *sh* sound, for example), hard consonants such as *k* and *t*, and spitting plosive sounds (such as the *p* in *crap*).

Whether or not the *sh* sound makes a word more foul, it's clear that some words rub people the wrong way. Here are words and phrases that will provoke the most horrified and appalled responses from friends, coworkers, and family (e.g., "Did you actually just say the word cunt out loud?? I can't believe you just said the C word").

ass face
ass hat
ass monkey
ass muncher
cock sucker
cum junkie
cunt
cunt face
cunt waffle
dick breath
dick head
dick wad
douche
douche face
fuck bag
fuck face
fuck nut
fuck you, you fucking fuck
fuckity fuck fuck
fucktard
fudge packer
gaytarded
ho
lard ass
mother fucker
pussy
twat
wanker

shown that most people are uncomfortable saying "fuck" in a public setting among strangers (milder words or euphemisms are preferred, such as "screwing" or "doing the nasty"). Yet these very same people are completely comfortable saying "fuck" to intimate friends and to their own sexual partners.

All of which means two things: Swearing is more common than you might think, and there's no such thing as an absolutely taboo swear word. The very same word may come across as vulgar and offensive, or as rip-roaringly funny, depending on the social context. The most famous example here is the word *nigger*. It's about as offensive as it can be when uttered by a white person. But not so if uttered by a black person or even by some ethnic groups (think of Asian and Hispanic rappers calling each other "nigger"). Once again, intention and context are everything.

THE IMPORTANCE OF BEING RUDE

Interrupting people is rude. Talking over people is rude. Being condescending is rude.

Yet these are all run-of-the-mill examples of rudeness. To be truly and exceptionally rude, you must intentionally disregard societal norms. You're being exceptionally rude when you blatantly disregard the accepted behavior of any group or culture.

The jokes in this book are rude, and intentionally so. These jokes don't simply use the wrong fork, yell when they should whisper, or generally embarrass themselves by not knowing the rules of the game.

No, the jokes in this book know exactly what they are doing. They yell, push, and shove because sometimes it is important to be rude. No glossing over tough topics and taboo subjects; no ignoring whatever elephant lurks in the corner; no suppressing feelings or emotions that have no other escape valve. Like swearing, rudeness can be cathartic. Rudeness is also a great way to shine a spotlight on the conscious (and subconscious) prejudices people share.

So go ahead, be a little rude. You may just learn something telling about yourself and your peer group.

A VERY BRIEF HISTORY OF JOKE BOOKS

It's said that the world's oldest profession is prostitution and the second-oldest is politics. Perhaps the third-oldest profession is joke telling. References to jokes go back to the very beginning of written history.

The godfather of comedy is Crates, a fifth-century Greek playwright who penned the world's first one-liners. The ancient Greeks, in fact, were serious about their jokes. In Athens the Group of Sixty, a club of and for local comedians, met regularly to exchange jokes (Philip of Macedon supposedly paid to have the group's jokes written down; sadly the book has not survived.)

The Roman playwright Plautus refers to "books of jest" in his plays, and the Roman scholar Melissus is said to have authored dozens of joke anthologies. Unfortunately there's only a single surviving example of these ancient joke books. The *Philogelos* (Laughter Lover) is a fifth-century c.e. collection of Greek jokes that, somewhat shockingly, still tickles the funny bone even today.

Europe completely lost its sense of humor during the Dark Ages. Fortunately, the art of joke telling survived in the Arab world; over the course of the Crusades, the concept of written humor filtered slowly back into Western consciousness.

The rebirth, so to speak, of Western joke anthologies came in the late fourteenth century courtesy of an Italian, Poggio Bracciolini, secretary to eight early Renaissance popes.

Bracciolini traveled across Europe searching for lost works of literature yet history remembers him mostly for his lone joke book, *Liber Facetiarum*. This short collection of jokes was the first of its kind to be published in Europe. When it hit the shelves in 1452, filled with political jokes and ribald tales of lusty church officials, it was an instant hit.

In Elizabethan England, writers such as Christopher Marlowe, Francis Bacon, and William Shakespeare took the funny stories of past ages and transformed them, in printed form, into something that you'd instantly recognize as a joke. The hallmarks of Elizabethan humor are still with us today: wit, satire, double entendre, and the buildup to a punch line.

The birth of dirty joke anthologies—from professors and editors with an appreciation for dirty joke scholarship—came in the nineteenth century, with lusty titles such as *La Fleur Lascive Oriental* (The Lascivious Oriental Flower; 1882) and *Contes Licencieux de Constantinople et de l'Asie Mineur* (Licentious Tales of Constantinople and Asia Minor; 1893).

By the 1950s and '60s in the United States, joke books had gone mainstream. Anthologies such as Leo Guild's *Bachelor's Joke Book (For Laughs and Relaxation)* and *Playboy's Party Jokes (Hundreds of Sophisticated Laughs from America's Most Sophisticated Magazine)* ushered in the golden era of mass-market joke books.

2

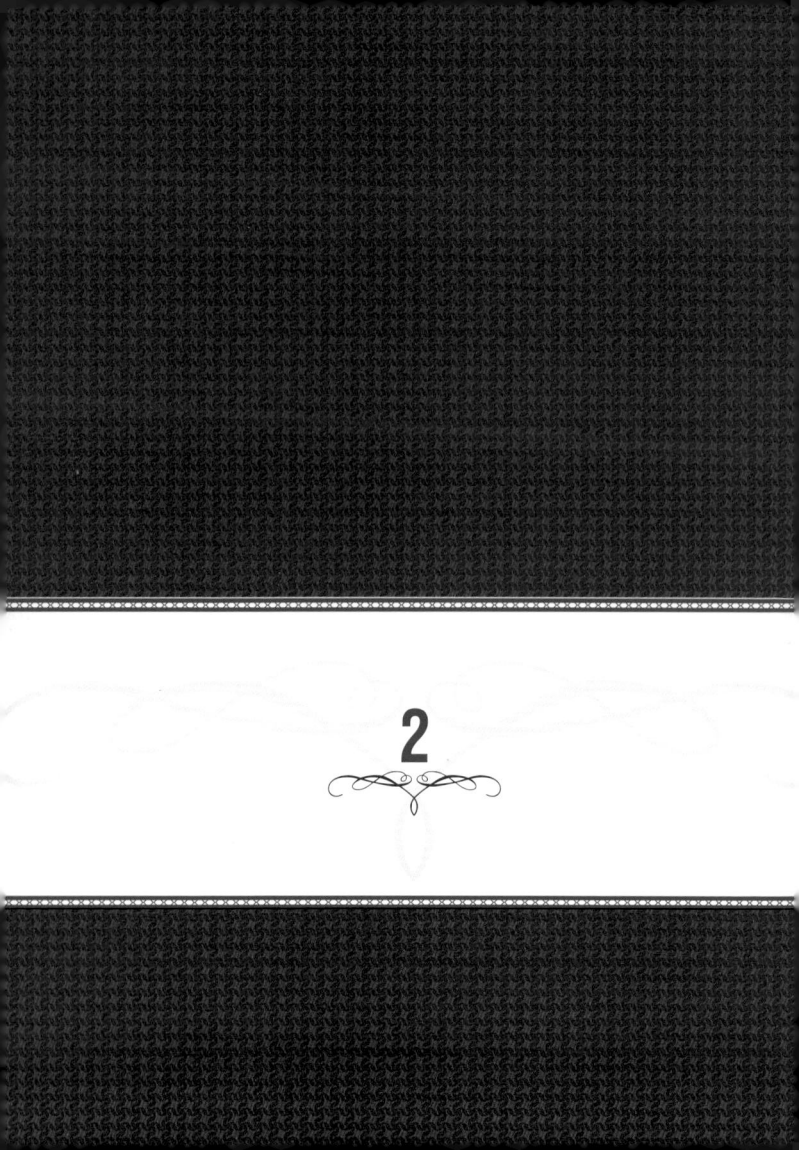

RUDE "DIFFERENTLY ABLED"

The blind, the lame, and the dumb—what a bunch of idiots. We kick off the *Classic Book of Rude Jokes* poking fun at people who least deserve it, and who are the least equipped to protest. Bravo!

A blind boy is being tucked into bed by his mother. "Honey," his mom says, "I want you to pray really hard tonight so that tomorrow, your wishes will come true!"

The next morning the boy wakes up and screams, "Mommy! My wish didn't come true. I'm still blind."

"I know," his mom replies. "Ha-ha–April fool!"

Q: How many deaf people does it take to screw in a light bulb?
A: None. They all just sit in the dark and cry.

Q: What's better than winning the Special Olympics?
A: Having arms and legs.

Q: What's better than winning the Special Olympics?
A: Not being "special."

Q: How did the blind kid burn the side of his face?
A: He answered the iron.

Q: How did he burn the other side?
A: They called back.

Q: Why don't blind people skydive?
A: It scares the hell out of their dogs.

Q: How does a blind skydiver know when to pull the cord?
A: The leash goes slack.

Q: Why did Helen Keller cross the road?
A: What, you think she has *any idea* where she is going?

Q: What did Helen Keller do when she fell down the stairs?
A: Screamed her hands off.

Q: Why was Helen Keller's leg yellow?
A: Her dog was blind, too.

Q: What did Helen Keller's parents do to punish her for swearing?
A: They washed her hands with soap.

Q: Why did Helen Keller's dog jump off the cliff?
A: You would, too, if your name was mmmmmmmnnnnnnnpf.

Q: Why were Helen Keller's hands purple?
A: She heard it through the grapevine.

Q: What does Helen Keller call her closet?
A: Disneyland!

Q: How did Helen Keller burn her hands?
A: Reading a waffle iron.

Q: What is Helen Keller's favorite color?
A: Corduroy.

Q: If Helen Keller fell down in the woods, would she make a sound?
A: . . .

Q: Why can't Helen Keller drive?
A: Because she's dead.

Helen Keller, Whipping Girl of Blind Jokes

Helen Keller was born in Alabama in 1880 and died in 1968 (*not* from reading a waffle iron). Despite being both deaf and blind, Helen learned to sign and became a prolific author and scholar, and an antiwar protester.

While nobody knows who told the first joke about Helen Keller, by the early 1980s Helen Keller joke lists went viral thanks to mass-market joke books such as *Truly Tasteless Jokes* (which hit the *New York Times* bestseller list, believe it or not).

Q: Why did the boy fall off the swing?
A: He didn't have any arms.

Q: How do you get a moron out of a tree?
A: Wave.

Q: How do you make a moron laugh on Saturday?
A: Tell him a joke on Wednesday.

Q: Why do morons work seven days a week?
A: So you don't have to retrain them on Monday.

Q: Why did the moron hit his head against the wall?
A: Because it felt so good when he stopped.

Q: How do you get a moron to commit suicide?
A: Put a knife in his hand and ask, "Who's special?"

Two morons are at a train station. The first moron asks the clerk, "Can I take this train to Chicago?"

"No," the clerk replies.

"Can I?" asks the other.

Q: What goes "Click-click-click . . . Did I get it?"
A: Stevie Wonder doing a Rubik's Cube.

Q: How did Stevie Wonder meet his wife?
A: Blind date.

Q: Why can't Stevie Wonder read?
A: Because he's black.

Q: What do you call a tennis match between Stevie Wonder and Helen Keller?
A: Endless love.

Q: What's the opposite of Christopher Reeve?
A: Christopher Walken.

Q: How many sugars does Christopher Reeve take in his coffee?
A: *Blinks twice*

Q: Christopher Reeve walks into a bar . . .
A: LOL

Q: What's the difference between Christopher Reeve and O. J. Simpson?
A: Christopher Reeve got the electric chair.

Top Five I.Q.-Challenged Movies

WHAT'S EATING GILBERT GRAPE? (1993)
Leonardo DiCaprio earns top marks for his portrayal of a clueless, witless dolt who loves his grossly obese chain-smoking mother. Best line from the movie: "I'm having a party, and you're not invited!"

FORREST GUMP (1994)
The film earned a healthy $667 million worldwide at the box office and garnered actor Tom Hanks a permanent spot on the low IQ list. Best line from the movie: "Stupid is as stupid does."

SLING BLADE (1996)
Billy Bob Thornton plays simple-minded Karl Childers, released back to his hometown after twenty years in a mental ward for—spoiler alert!—killing his own mother. Best line from the movie: "Mmm hmm."

RAIN MAN (1988)

Tom Cruise plays the mean older brother. Dustin Hoffman plays the estranged idiot-savant younger brother, with a three-million-dollar inheritance and a knack for counting cards. Hello, Las Vegas foibles! Best line from the movie: "Uh-oh, fart."

THERE'S SOMETHING ABOUT MARY (1998)

The Farrelly brothers' best film (don't argue about this) features the inimitable Warren Jensen, the dim-witted brother of Cameron Diaz's Mary Jensen. Warren at the batting cages, Warren on a go-kart, Warren when Ben Stiller is being stretchered out to an ambulance . . . hilarious. Best line from the movie: "Franks and beans! Franks and beans!"

Q: What one good thing came from Christopher Reeve's death?
A: Stephen Hawking got his parking space back.

A blind man is sitting on a park bench. A rabbi sits down next to him eating a piece of matzoh. Taking pity on the blind man, the rabbi breaks off a piece and gives it to him. Several minutes later the blind man turns to the rabbi and asks, "Who wrote this crap?"

Q: What do you call a guy with no arms and no legs in a pile of leaves?
A: Russell.

Q: What do you call a guy with no arms and no legs in the ocean?
A: Bob.

Q: What do you call that same guy two weeks later?
A: Fish food.

Q: What do you call a guy with no arms and no legs in a forest fire?
A: Bernie.

Q: What do you call a guy with no arms and no legs hanging on the wall?
A: Art.

Q: What do you call a guy with no arms and no legs on your front steps?
A: Matt.

Q: What do you call a dog with no arms and no legs?
A: It doesn't matter, he won't come.

Q: What do you call a cat with no arms and no legs?
A: Dog food.

Q: What do you call a girl with one arm and one leg?
A: Eileen.

Q: What do you call a Chinese girl with one leg?
A: Irene.

Q: What do you call a girl with no arms and no legs sitting on a grill?
A: Patty.

Q: What do you call a guy with no arms and no legs sitting on a grill?
A: Frank.

Q: What do you call an electrician with no arms and no legs?
A: Sparky.

Q: What do you call a guy with no arms and no legs covered in oil?
A: Derek.

Q: What do you call a guy with no arms and no legs resting on a podium?
A: Mike.

Q: What do you call a guy with no arms and no legs on hot pavement?
A: Flip.

Q: What do you call a guy with no arms and no legs under a car?
A: Jack.

Q: What do you call two guys with no arms and no legs hanging from a window?
A: Curt and Rod.

Q: What do you call a guy with no arms and no legs in a tiger cage?
A: Claude.

Q: What do you call a guy with no arms and no legs in your mailbox?
A: Bill.

Q: What do you call a guy with no arms and no legs riding a roller coaster?
A: Ralph.

Q: What do you call a girl with no arms and no legs who feels worthless?
A: Penny.

Q: What do you call a guy with no arms and no legs covered in sauerkraut?
A: Reuben.

Q: What do you call a girl with no arms and no legs on a tennis court?
A: Annette.

Q: What do you call a guy with no arms and no legs on a golf course?
A: Chip.

Q: What do you call a guy with no arms and no legs caught in a meat grinder?
A: Chuck.

Q: What do you call a woman with no arms and no legs who gives good blow jobs?
A: Partially disabled.

Two strangers walk toward each other down the street, each dragging his left leg. One man looks down sorrowfully at his leg and says to the passing stranger, "Vietnam, 1968."

The other man says, "Dog shit, half a block back."

Q: Why did God make farts smell?
A: So deaf people could enjoy them, too.

Q: What do you call it when deaf people write their names on the back of their shirt collars?
A: Clothes captioning.

Q: What did the blind, deaf, mute quadriplegic kid get for his birthday?
A: A pinball machine.

Q: What did the blind, deaf, mute quadriplegic kid get for Christmas?
A: Cancer.

Q: Why do deaf mutes masturbate with one hand?
A: So they can moan with the other one.

Q: What do you get when an epileptic falls into a lettuce patch?
A: Seizure salad.

Q: What do you call an epileptic holding a glass of milk?
A: Milk shake.

Q: What do you throw to an epileptic who's having a fit in the bath?
A: Your laundry.

Q: What do you call an epileptic in a wheelchair?
A: A transformer.

Two brothers were opening presents at Christmas. The younger brother unwrapped a dozen presents while the older brother unwrapped just one. Feeling superior, the younger brother taunted the older one, "Ha-ha! I got twelve presents, and you only have one!"

The older brother replied, "Ha-ha, you have a brain tumor."

Q: How do you know when the vegetables are done?
A: The wheelchairs float to the top.

Q: Did you hear about the dyslexic lawyer?
A: He studied all year for the bra exam.

Q: Did you hear about the dyslexic pimp?
A: He bought a warehouse.

Q: Did you hear about the dyslexic devil worshiper?
A: He sacrificed his mom to Santa.

Q: A dyslexic asks his friend, "Can you smell gas?"
A: "No," the friend replies, "I can't even smell my own name."

Q: What's the best thing about being schizophrenic?
A: It turns masturbation into an orgy.

Q: What happens when a schizophrenic takes an acid trip?
A: Nothing. But it can be a nice distraction.

3

RUDE BLONDES

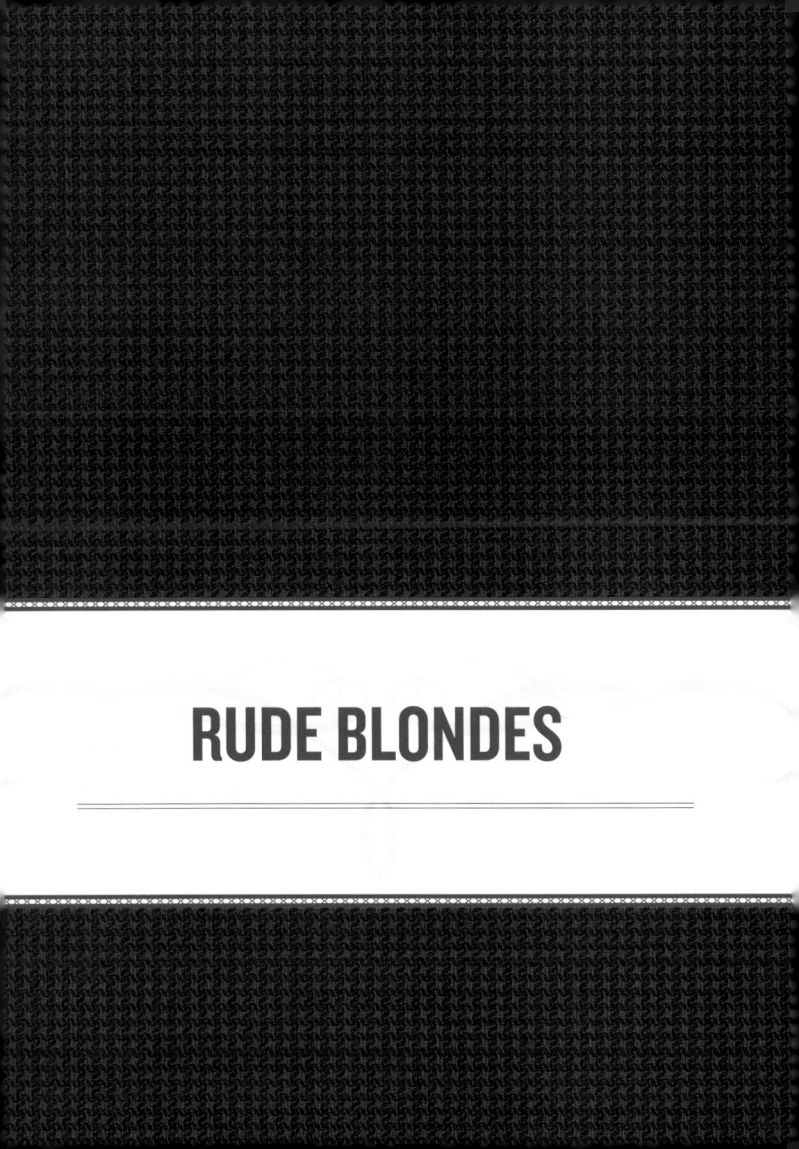

ARE BLONDES DUMBER THAN EVERYBODY ELSE? BELIEVE IT OR NOT, SERIOUS PEOPLE WITH PhDS HAVE STUDIED THE INTELLIGENCE OF BLONDES VERSUS REDHEADS AND BRUNETTES. AND THE ANSWER FROM SCIENCE IS—NO! BLONDES ARE NEITHER SMARTER NOR DUMBER THAN THE REST OF HUMANITY. THEY'RE EQUALLY SMART (OR EQUALLY DUMB, DEPENDING ON HOW FULL OF WATER YOUR GLASS IS).

Which begs the question, Do blondes actually have more fun? The answer is an emphatic, "Way to go, team!"

Q: How do you confuse a blonde?
A: You don't. They're born that way.

Q: What do you call a blonde behind a steering wheel?
A: Air bag.

Q: Why do blondes like convertibles?
A: More legroom.

Q: Why is it good to have a blonde passenger?
A: You get to park in the handicapped zone.

Q: What's blonde, brunette, blonde, brunette?
A: A blonde doing cartwheels.

Q: What do you call it when a blonde dyes her hair brunette?
A: Artificial intelligence.

Q: What do you get when you turn a blonde upside down?
A: A brunette with bad breath.

Q: How do you get a blonde to marry you?
A: Tell her she is pregnant.

Q: What will she ask you?
A: "Is it mine?"

Q: Why did the blonde climb over the glass wall?
A: To see what was on the other side.

Q: How did the blonde break her nose?
A: Somebody put a dildo under a glass table.

Q: Why did God give blondes 2 percent more brains than horses?
A: Because God didn't want them shitting on the street during parades.

Q: How many blondes does it take to change a light bulb?
A: Two. One to hold the Diet Coke and one to shout, "Daaaddy!"

A blind man walks into a bar, makes his way to a bar stool and orders a drink. After sitting there for a while, he yells to the bartender, "Hey, you wanna hear a blonde joke?"

The bar falls absolutely quiet. In a very deep, husky voice the woman next to him says, "Before you tell that joke, sir, I think it's only fair that you should know five things: First, the bartender is a blonde girl with a baseball bat. Second, the bouncer is a blonde girl. Third, I'm a blonde with a black belt in karate. Fourth, the woman sitting next to me is a blonde and a professional boxer. Fifth, the lady to your right is a blonde and a decorated war veteran."

She puts her hand on the blind man's arm and says, "Now think about it seriously, mister. Do you still want to tell that blonde joke?"

The blind man thinks for a second, shakes his head and mutters, "Naw, not if I'm gonna have to explain it five fucking times."

Q: What's the mating call of the blonde?
A: "I am sooooo drunk!"

The Science of Natural Blondes

Did you know that, according to a study by the World Health Organization (WHO), natural blondes are likely to be extinct within two hundred years because there are too few people carrying the blonde gene? The last natural blonde is likely to be born in Finland in the 2200s.

Actually, this was a hoax. The WHO never commissioned a study on blondes. And yet in 2002 this fake story was plastered across the world's newspapers. Cynics believe it's all part of a long-established anti-blonde movement. It's just like magazine articles that claim men consider dark-haired women most desirable (not true—preference for hair color varies by culture).

And the latest (actual) scientific claim? In a twist, scientists have shown that men score lower on a general intelligence test after being shown pictures of blonde women! In a 2007 study, scientists found that men's mental performance dropped because they believed they were dealing with someone less intelligent.

So are blondes really dumb?

Nope. The problem is actually the men who look at them.

Q: What's the mating call of an ugly blonde?
A: "I said, I am sooooo drunk!"

Q: A blonde, a brunette, and a redhead are all in fifth grade. Who has the largest tits?
A: The blonde, because she's eighteen.

Q: What's the difference between a group of blondes and a good magician?
A: The magician has a cunning array of stunts.

Q: What's the difference between a blonde and the Panama Canal?
A: The Panama Canal is a busy ditch.

Q: Did you hear about the new blonde paint?
A: It's not real bright, but it's cheap and spreads easy.

Q: What did the blonde's left leg say to her right leg?
A: Between the two of us, we can make a lot of money.

Q: What's the difference between a blonde and the *Titanic*?
A: They know how many men went down on the *Titanic*.

Q: What's the difference between a blonde and a mosquito?
A: One stops sucking when you slap it.

Q: Why don't blondes use vibrators?
A: They chip their teeth.

A blonde tells her friend she is done with men forever. "They lie and cheat," she explains, "and they're just no good. From now on when I want sex, I'm going to use my vibrator."

"So, what will you do when the batteries run out?" her friend asks.

"I'll just fake an orgasm like always."

Q: Why is a blonde like a doorknob?
A: Because everyone gets a turn.

Q: What do blondes and computers have in common?
A: You never truly appreciate them until they go down on you.

Q: Why don't blondes talk when having sex?
A: Their mothers taught them not to talk with their mouths full.

Q: What's the difference between a blonde and a bowling ball?
A: You can only fit three fingers in a bowling ball.

Q: What does a blonde say after multiple orgasms?
A: "Way to go, team!"

Q: What's the difference between a blonde and a brick?
A: The brick doesn't follow you home after you have sex with it.

Q: What's a blonde's idea of safe sex?
A: Locking the car door.

Q: Why do blondes always turn on the lights after sex?
A: Eventually, the car door always opens.

Q: Why do blondes have big belly buttons?
A: From dating blond men.

Q: What do you call a blonde lesbian?
A: A waste.

Q: What's the difference between a blonde and your toothbrush?
A: You don't let your best friend borrow your toothbrush.

Q: What's the difference between a blonde and your job?
A: Your job still sucks after six months.

Playlist: Blondes

"Episode of Blonde" by Elvis Costello

"Suicide Blonde'" by INXS
(extra point for suicide irony)

"Lebanese Blonde" by Thievery Corporation

"Blonde" by The Wedding Present

"Blondes With Lobotomy Eyes"
by My Life with the Thrill Kill Kult

"Blondes Have More Fun" by Rod Stewart

"Joey" by Concrete Blonde

"One Way or Another" by Blondie

A ventriloquist is onstage at a small bar. He's going through his usual run of dumb blonde jokes when a large blonde in the second row stands up and shouts, "I've heard just about enough of your denigrating blonde jokes! What makes you think you can stereotype blondes that way? What does a person's physical attributes have to do with her worth as a human being?"

The ventriloquist looks on in confused amazement.

"It's jerks like you who keep women like me from being respected," she continues, "and from reaching my full potential as a person, because you perpetuate discrimination against not only blondes but women at large. All in the name of a few pathetic jokes."

Flustered, the ventriloquist begins to apologize.

The blonde interrupts, "You stay out of this, mister. I'm talking to that little fucker on your knee."

4

RUDE RELIGION

THERE'S SOMETHING INTRINSICALLY FUNNY ABOUT RELIGION. WHILE THERE'S NO MORE SERIOUS A TOPIC THAN GOD IN ALL HIS/HER MANY FORMS, THINGS LIKE DEVILS WITH POINTY TAILS, VESTAL VIRGINS IN PARADISE, PEDOPHILE PRIESTS, AND CARTOON JIHADS MAKE RELIGION A RIPE TOPIC FOR POKING WITH A FUN-STICK.

A priest is checking into a hotel and points to a sign on the desk that reads:

> *Each room contains:*
> *Comfortable king-sized bed*
> *Air conditioning*
> *Coffeepot*
> *Color TV with adult entertainment*

The priest says to the clerk, "I hope the pornography in my room is disabled."

The clerk replies, "No, we just have regular porn, you sick fuck."

Q: How do you get a nun pregnant?
A: Dress her up as an altar boy.

Q: How do you get a nun pregnant?
A: Fuck her.

Q: How many Catholic priests does it take to screw in a light bulb?
A: Two. One to screw the light bulb and the other to screw the altar boy.

Q: What's the difference between a Catholic priest and a pimple?
A: A pimple waits until puberty before coming on your face.

Q: How is the Bible like a penis?
A: Both are forced down your throat by priests.

Q: What's white and rains down from the heavens?
A: The coming of Christ.

A priest and a rabbi are walking down the street when they pass a playground. The priest says to the rabbi, "You wanna screw those kids?"

The rabbi asks, "Out of what?"

Hallelujah: Tasteless Jesus Jokes

Jesus walks into a hotel, tosses three nails on the front desk, and says, "Hey, can you put me up for the night?"

Why did Jesus cross the road?
Because he was nailed to the chicken.

What did Jesus say as he was being crucified?
Ahhhhhhhhhhh!

Take 2: What did Jesus say as he was being crucified?
Don't touch my fuckin' Easter eggs. I'll be back on Monday.

Jesus is hanging on the cross, and as his mother is below him, weeping, he looks down and says, "Mother, . . ."
"Yes?" she replies.
"I can see our house from here."

Jesus is coming. But did he pull out?

Sure, Jesus loves you. But does he swallow?

Q: How many Christians does it take to screw in a light bulb?
A: Two, but God only knows how they got in there.

Q: How many conservative Christians does it take to screw in a light bulb?
A: Five. One to change the bulb and four to testify it was lit from the moment they began screwing.

Q: How many Pentecostal Christians does it take to screw in a light bulb?
A: Ten. One to change the bulb, nine to pray against the Lord of Darkness.

Q: How many Christian Scientists does it take to screw in a light bulb?
A: Zero, though it takes at least one to sit and pray for the old one to go back on.

Q: How many Calvinist Christians does it take to screw in a light bulb?
A: Zero. God has predestined when the lights will be on.

Q: How many Lutheran Christians does it take to screw in a light bulb?
A: Zero. Sorry, but Lutherans don't believe in change.

Top Five Joke Religions

It's easy to make fun of Christians, Jews, and Muslims. You'll get a good laugh out of Buddhists and Mormons, too. Then there are those religions that are so damn weird, jokes kinda miss the point.

THE UNIVERSE PEOPLE. They live in the Czech Republic and believe that ancient nonearthly beings operate a fleet of spaceships orbiting the Earth. The Universe People followers are waiting to be transported into another dimension. Bon voyage, we say.

NUWAUBIANISM. It's a loose term referring to the religion founded by Dwight York, a black supremacist leader and convicted child molester (he's currently in prison serving a 135-year sentence). Some things the Nuwaubianists believe: All humans have seven clones living on different parts of the planet; humans were bred on Mars as part of a Homo erectus breeding program gone awry; and famed scientist Nikola Tesla was born on the planet Venus. Amen, brother.

RAJNEESHISM. Bhagwan Shree Rajneesh was an Indian-born mystic who eventually settled in the state of Oregon in the 1980s. The group's claims to religious fame? Preaching that Rolls-Royces were a sign of holiness (Rajneesh owned dozens of them) and trying to poison nonbelievers by introducing salmonella into salad bars in several Oregon fast-food restaurants. Their God was clearly an angry one.

THE CREATIVITY MOVEMENT. It's a white separatist movement advocating a white-only religion called Creativity. Ironically, despite their name, the group does not believe in God. Followers of The Creativity Movement are—wait for it—atheists!

HEAVEN'S GATE. A cult founded by Marshall Applewhite, whose followers believed that, once they were free of their earthly bodies, a spaceship would take them away to a celestial paradise. The 1997 appearance of the Hale-Bopp comet was a sign their spaceship had arrived. In March of that year, thirty-nine members of the cult were found dead in a mass suicide. Their bags were packed. They all wore running shoes and matching uniforms with patches that said "Heaven's Gate Away Team." Each had a $5 bill and a roll of quarters in their pockets. And no, you couldn't make this stuff up if you tried.

Q: How many atheists does it take to screw in a light bulb?
A: One. But they are still in darkness.

Jesus and God were playing golf. They come to a nasty par 4 with trees and water hazards everywhere. Jesus grabs his driver and hits a beautiful shot down the middle of the fairway.

God grabs a 2-iron and shanks one off a tree and into a pond.

All of a sudden there's a blinding flash of light and God's ball appears in the mouth of a fish, which swims to the surface and is speared in the talons of a mighty hawk flying overhead. The hawk flies above the green and the fish drops the ball from its mouth. The ball rolls to the pin and falls into the cup.

Jesus turns to God and says, "You gonna play golf, or you gonna fuck around?"

Q: How many Chassidim does it take to change a light bulb?
A: None. They will never find one that burned as brightly as the first one.

Q: How many Jewish mothers does it take the change a light bulb?
A: "No, please don't bother, I'll sit in the dark. I don't want to be a nuisance to anybody."

Q: Why don't Jewish mothers drink?
A: Alcohol interferes with their suffering.

Q: What did the waiter ask the group of Jewish mothers?
A: "Is anything okay?"

Q: What did the Jewish grandmother bank teller say to her customer?
A: "You never write, you never call. You only come to see me when you need money."

A Jewish man was talking to his psychiatrist. "I had a weird dream recently. I saw my mother, but then I noticed she had your face. It was so disturbing I couldn't fall back asleep. I just lay there staring at the ceiling, thinking about it until seven in the morning. I finally got up, made myself a slice of toast and some coffee, and came straight here. Can you please help me explain the meaning of my dream?"

The psychiatrist kept silent for some time and then said, "One slice of toast and coffee? You call that a breakfast?"

Q: What happened when the Jewish man walked into the wall with a hard-on?
A: He broke his nose.

A Jewish man was hit by a car and knocked down. The paramedics arrived and eased him onto a stretcher in the ambulance. "Are you comfortable?" the paramedic asked.

"I make a good living," the man replied.

Q: Why do Jewish men watch porn films backward?
A: They love the bit where the prostitute gives back the money.

Q: How does a Jewish wife cheat on her husband?
A: She has a headache with the pool man.

Q: What's the technical term for a divorced Jewish woman?
A: Plaintiff.

Q: What's a Jewish woman's idea of natural childbirth?
A: No makeup, whatsoever.

Q: How many Jewish wives does it take to change a light bulb?
A: None. Jewish wives don't change light bulbs.

Q: What three words will a Jewish wife never hear?
A: "Attention, Walmart shoppers...."

An older Jewish man moves into an old age home but is just as horny as ever. As he looks over the list of the other people living in the home, he realizes there are three times as many women as men. The man decides this is a good opportunity to make some money, so he posts a sign on his door that reads: **SEX FOR SALE.**

On the very first night, someone knocks on his door. An elderly woman asks, "What does your sign mean?"

"I am selling sex," he replies.

"Well, how much do you charge?"

The man replies, "I haven't thought much about prices, but I suppose it will be five dollars on the floor, ten dollars on the chair, or twenty dollars on the bed."

The elderly woman reaches into her purse and pulls out a twenty-dollar bill.

"Oh, you want it on the bed?" he asks.

"No," she says. "Four on the floor, please!"

Two married Jewish women are having lunch. One complains that every time she and her husband have sex, he screams and yells when he climaxes.

"So what's wrong with that?" the friend asks.

Her friend replies, "Are you kidding, the screaming always wakes me up!"

Q: How does a Jewish pedophile hunt for little boys?
A: "Hey kid, want to buy some candy?"

Q: What does a Jewish pedophile say to the little boy once he's in the car?
A: "Hey kid, go easy on the sweets."

Q: Did you hear about the Jewish Santa Claus?
A: He comes down the chimney and says, "Hi kids! You want to buy some presents?"

Q: How can you tell a Jewish house at Christmas?
A: There's a parking meter on the roof.

Q: A Jew asks his rabbi, "Why did God create gentiles?"
A: "Well," the rabbi said, "somebody has got to buy retail."

A Jewish man is talking to God and asks, "God, how long is a million years?"

God answers, "To me, it's about a minute."

"God, how much is a million dollars?"

"To me, it's a penny."

"God, may I have a penny?"

"Wait a minute."

A young boy approached his father at the end of his first day of Hebrew school. "Father, I need five dollars to buy a used textbook for school."

"Four dollars?" the father replied. "What do you need three dollars for?"

Q: What do you get when you cross a kleptomaniac and a Mormon?
A: A basement full of stolen food.

Q: What do you get when you mix LSD and LDS?
A: A high priest.

A Jewish man, a Catholic man, and a Mormon man were having drinks at the bar following a business meeting. The Jewish man, bragging about his virility, said, "I have four strong sons. One more and I'll have a basketball team!"

The Catholic man was not impressed. "That's nothing. I have ten sons. One more and I'll have a football team."

To which the Mormon replied, "Gentlemen, I have seventeen wives. One more and I'll have a golf course!"

Q: What's the difference between a virtuous Mormon and a sinful Mormon?
A: The temperature of the caffeine they drink.

Q: Why do you always take two Mormons with you when you go fishing?
A: If you take only one, he'll drink all your beer.

Q: What's great about being a Mormon and living in Tennessee?
A: You can marry *all* your cousins.

Q: Why do Mormon women stop having babies at thirty-five?
A: Because thirty-six is just too damn many.

A Mormon father, giving marital advice to his son, says there are five important qualities to look for in a woman.

"First," the dad says, "you must find a woman who can cook, clean, and look after the kids."

"Second, you must find a woman who is dirty in bed and loves having sex."

"Third, you must find a woman who has a lot in common with you, so you can have a good laugh and talk about life."

"Fourth, you must find a woman who has plenty of money to look after you to the standard you are accustomed to."

"And finally," the dad says, "and this is very, very, very important: Never, under any circumstances, must these four women meet!"

A man walks into a sex shop in Jerusalem looking for a sex doll. The clerk asks, "So what kind do you want, Jewish or Muslim?"

The man looks confused and asks, "What's the difference?"

"The Muslim one blows itself up."

Top Five Weird Mormon Beliefs

1. Mormons can drink coffee—as long as it's cold. Mormons believe "hot drinks are not for the body or belly," so caffeine is limited to the chilled variety.

2. Jesus's passport has a USA stamp. The Book of Mormon is meant to be contemporaneous with the Bible. And after Jesus's resurrection, according to Mormons, Jesus came to America and visited the two tribes of Mormons.

3. Mormon priests can only be male. Women are forbidden. Interestingly, a "revelation"' (a.k.a., "pending lawsuit"?) allowed black men to become Mormon priests in 1978.

4. Multiple Gods, multiple worlds. Mormons believe that God created multiple worlds and each world has people just like us living on it. They also believe that multiple Gods exist, each with his own universe.

5. Mormon men can have multiple wives in heaven. High five for celestial polygamy.

Two Muslim men are talking on a street corner. One shows the other a picture and says, "This is my first son. He's a martyr."

He shows the man another picture and says, "This is my second son. He's a martyr."

He shows the man another picture and says, "This is my third son. He's going to be a martyr."

The other man replies, "Yes, they blow up so fast these days."

Q: What did the Muslim woman say to her husband?
A: "Does my bomb look big in this?"

Q: What's the difference between a Western girl and a Muslim girl?
A: The Western girl gets stoned before she commits adultery.

Q: How do you know when a Muslim boy becomes a man?
A: His diaper moves from his butt to his head.

Q: What's the title of Salman Rushdie's latest book?
A: *Buddha, You Fat Bastard.*

Q: Take 2: What's the title of Salman Rushdie's latest book?
A: *Jesus Was a Lousy Carpenter.*

A Muslim suicide bomber walks into a crowd of infidels and blows himself up. He is immediately transported to Paradise, where he finds himself surrounded by seventy-two of the ugliest women anyone has ever laid eyes upon.

The suicide bomber is crestfallen. Allah pats him sympathetically on the shoulder and says, "C'mon, think it through. Why do you think they're all still virgins?"

An Arab man is walking through customs at an airport. The customs agent looks at his passport and asks, "Sex?"

"Yes, please!" the Arab man says.

"No, I mean male or female," replies the agent.

"Both. And sometimes camels, too!"

An Arab man dies and arrives at Heaven's Pearly Gates. Saint Peter asks, "Yes, how can I help?"

"I'm here to meet Jesus," the man says.

Saint Peter looks over his shoulder and shouts, "Jesus, your taxi is here!"

There's already been some trouble for Osama bin Laden in the afterlife. There was a mix-up and he was mistakenly greeted by seventy-two vegans.

Q: What's the biggest problem with being an atheist?
A: Nobody to talk to during an orgasm.

Q: Why did the atheist cross the road?
A: He thought there might be a street on the other side, but he wouldn't believe it until he tested the hypothesis.

Q: What do you get when you cross an atheist with a Jehovah's Witness?
A: Somebody knocking on your door for no apparent reason.

5

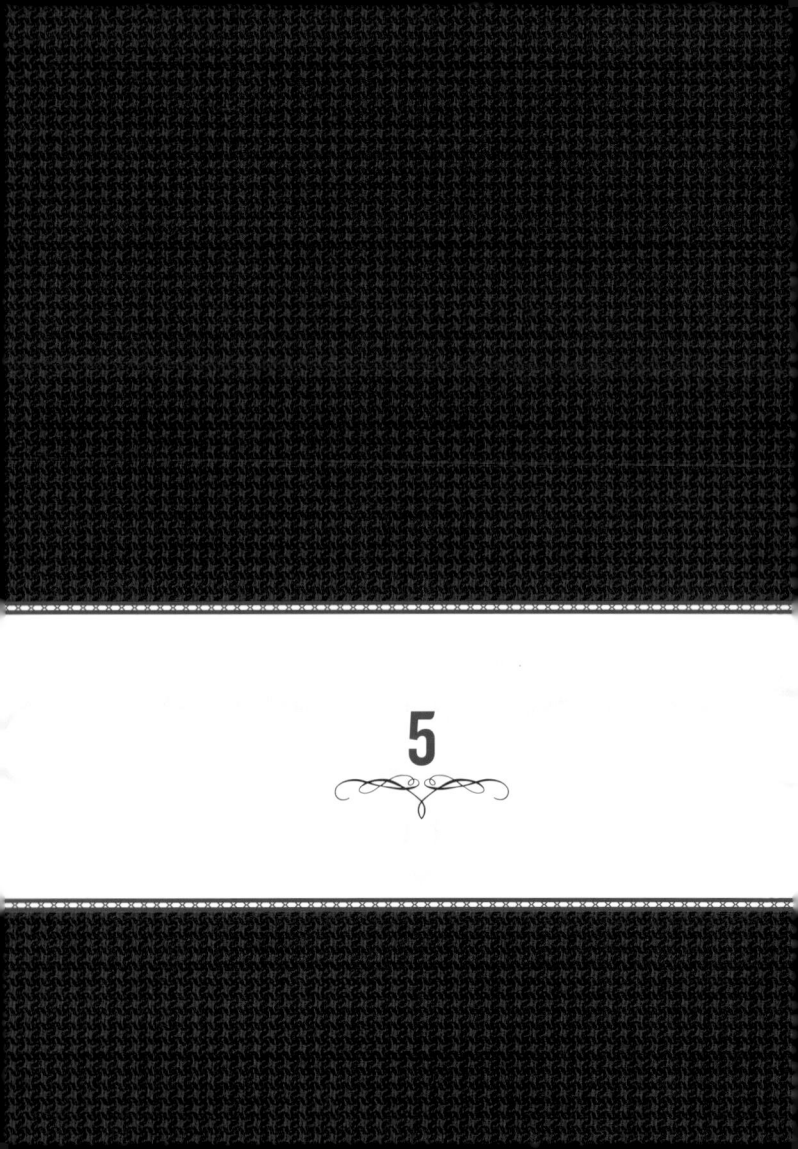

RUDE RACISTS

MAINSTREAM AMERICA HAS LONG GREETED IMMIGRANTS WITH ANIMOSITY AND SUSPICION—AND MADE THEM THE TARGETS OF RACIALLY CHARGED HUMOR. WE POKE FUN AT THEIR ACCENTS, CUISINE, DRESS, AND CULTURE. LIKE IT OR NOT, RACIST JOKES ARE AN AMERICAN TRADITION.

Over time these "foreigners" blend comfortably into the American melting pot; as they do, a fresh wave of first-generation immigrants takes their place as the butt of the same old jokes. Once it was Chinese railroad workers, then it was the Irish (believe it or not, there was a time when "No Irish Need Apply" signs were ubiquitous at New York City construction sites), Italians, Poles, Jews, Russians, Mexicans, Vietnamese, Cubans, Arabs; the list goes on and on.

A Chinese couple get married. The new bride is a virgin, and on the wedding night she cowers naked under the sheets as her husband undresses. He climbs in next to her and tries to be reassuring, "My dar-ring, I know dis you firt time and you flighten . . . I plomise you, I give you anyting you want, I do anyting you want. What you want?"

She smiles coyly and says, "I wan' numma sixty-nine."

"You wan' beef with bloccoli now?"

Q: What do you call "69" in Chinese?
A: Two Can Chew.

Q: What do you call a gay Chinese man?
A: Chew Man Chew.

Q: What do you call a Chinese child molester?
A: Fuckum Yung.

Q: What did the Chinese couple name their special-needs baby?
A: Sum Ting Wong.

Q: Why is there no Disneyland in China?
A: No one's tall enough to go on the rides.

Q: Why can't Chinese barbecue?
A: Because the rice falls through the grill.

Q: What do you call a fat Chinaman?
A: A chunk.

Q: What does a Chinese man do when he has an erection?
A: He votes.

Three brothers living in China want to immigrate to the United States. The brothers are named Bu, Chu, and Fu. So they decide to change their names to seem more American. Bu changed his name to Buck. Chu changed his name to Chuck. And Fu got sent back to China.

Q: How do you stop a French tank?
A: Say, "Boo."

Q: What is the difference between American fries and French fries?
A: Courage.

Q: After a recent terrorist bombing, what happened to the French terror-alert level?
A: It was raised from "run" to "hide." (The only higher levels are "surrender" and "collaborate.")

Q: Why do the French smell?
A: So blind people can hate them, too.

Q: What is the difference between a Frenchwoman and a basketball team?
A: The basketball team showers after four periods.

Q: What's the difference between an Irish wedding and an Irish wake?
A: One less drunk.

Q: Why did God invent whiskey?
A: So the Irish would never rule the world.

Q: Why can't Irishmen ever be lawyers?
A: They can never make it past the bar.

Q: How does an Irishman know his wife is dead?
A: The sex is the same, but the dishes start piling up.

Q: Why do Scotsmen wear kilts?
A: So the sheep won't hear the zip.

Q: Why do bagpipers walk when they play?
A: They're trying to get away from the noise.

Q: Why do bagpipers walk when they play?
A: A moving target is harder to hit.

A man walks into a bar with an octopus. He sits the octopus down on a stool and tells everyone in the bar, "This is the world's most talented octopus. He can play any musical instrument you can produce. In fact, I'll wager a hundred dollars that nobody here has an instrument this octopus cannot play."

Somebody in the bar pulls out a guitar. Immediately the octopus picks up the guitar and plays a rip-roaring guitar solo. The man pays up his hundred dollars.

Next somebody produces a trumpet. The octopus grabs the horn and plays a sweet melody. The man pays up his hundred dollars.

Then a Scotsman pulls out his bagpipes. The octopus fumbles with the pipes and has a confused look.

"Ha!" the Scotsman says, "Ye cannae plae it, can ye, octopus?"

The octopus looks up at him and says, "Play it? I'm going to fuck it as soon as I figure out how to remove its plaid pajamas."

Q: What's an Australian's idea of foreplay?
A: "You awake?"

Q: What's a Tasmanian's idea of foreplay?
A: "You awake, mum?"

Q: What does an Aussie girl use for protection during sex?
A: A bus shelter.

Two Afghan men are chatting in line, waiting to finalize their Australian residential status. They strike up a friendship and agree to meet in a year to see who has better adapted to the Australian way of life.

A year later, true to their word, they meet. The first man says to the second, "We've integrated completely. Yesterday I ate a meat pie with brown sauce, drank a cold VB, and watched my son play a game of footy with local kids."

The second man replies, "Fuck off, towelhead."

Q: Why do New Zealanders love rowing so much?
A: Because they get to sit down and go backward.

Q: What do you call a Kiwi with a sheep under each arm?
A: A pimp.

Q: How does a Kiwi find a sheep in tall grass?
A: Very satisfying.

Q: What do you call a Kiwi with a goat under one arm and a sheep under the other?
A: Bisexual.

A Greek and an Italian are drinking coffee, arguing over whose culture is superior. The Greek says, "We have the Parthenon."

"Sure," the Italian replies, "and we have the Coliseum."

"We Greeks gave birth to mathematics."

The Italian nods and says, "Sure, and we built the Roman Empire."

The Greek thinks for a moment and says, "Well, we invented sex."

"That is true," the Italian replies, "but it was the Italians who introduced it to women."

Q: Why do Italian men have moustaches?
A: So they can look more like their mammas.

Q: Why did the Italian man spit on his girlfriend's face?
A: To extinguish the fire in her moustache.

Q: Why do Italians wear gold chains around their necks?
A: So they know where to stop shaving.

Q: What's the difference between an Italian girl and a pizza?
A: There's less cheese on the pizza.

Q: What did the barber say to the Italian kid?
A: "Do you want your hair cut or should I just change the oil?"

Q: Why don't Italians have freckles?
A: They keep sliding off.

A Polish man was suffering from constipation, so his doctor prescribed suppositories. A week later the Pole complained to the doctor that they didn't produce the desired results. "Have you been taking them regularly?" the doctor asked.

"What do you think I've been doing," the Pole replied, "shoving them up my ass?"

Q: What happens when a Pole doesn't pay his garbage bill?
A: They stop delivering.

Q: Why can't Polish farmers raise chickens?
A: They plant the eggs too deep.

Why Do We Hate the Polaks?

First of all, let's get the spelling straight. It's not "Pollock" or "Polok" or "Polack"—it's plain old "Polak," which specifically refers to a male Polish person (a female Pole is known as a Polka, no joke). *Polak* is how the Polish spell it, so if we're going to make fun of them, we should at least spell the word properly.

Polak jokes play on two well-worn themes: that Poles are stupid and that the Polish race is somehow impure (thank the Nazis for this misconception). The Polak jokes familiar to most Americans date from the 1950s and '60s, when Polish immigration to the West caused friction with local workers who felt threatened by the influx of cheap unskilled labor from communist Poland.

And that's a point to remember, in case you're offended by the racist tone of these jokes. In many ways the Polaks wandered haplessly into these rude jokes. There's nothing "Polish" in these jokes and very little to illuminate Polish history or culture. Instead, these jokes capture a moment in time when middle-class America felt threatened by yet another wave of poor immigrants competing for jobs.

The good news, for Polaks at least, is that these jokes don't resonate with younger Americans. Kids these days don't remember the Polish influx, and they don't watch old episodes of *All in the Family* (Archie Bunker loved his Polak jokes). Thus the Polak joke begins its slow journey from mainstream to obscure. *Do widzenia!*

Q: What does it say on the bottom of Polish Coke bottles?
A: "Open other end."

Q: Heard about the Polish abortion clinic?
A: There's a twelve-month waiting list.

Q: How many Polaks does it take to change a light bulb?
A: Three. One to stand on a chair and hold the bulb, plus two to spin the chair.

Q: How do you ruin a Polish party?
A: Flush the punch bowl.

Q: What is long and hard and given to a Polish bride on her wedding night?
A: A new last name.

Q: How can you tell a Polish woman is having her period?
A: She's only wearing one sock.

Q: What's the Polish version of a vibrator?
A: A mop handle and six relatives shaking the bed.

Q: How many rednecks does it take to change a light bulb?
A: Three. One to hold the bulb and two to turn the ladder.

Q: What do a redneck divorce and a tornado have in common?
A: No matter what, somebody's losing a trailer.

Q: What do you get if you play country music backward?
A: You get your wife back, your kids back, your house back, your truck back . . .

Q: What's the difference between a good ol' boy and a redneck?
A: The good ol' boy raises livestock. The redneck gets emotionally involved.

Q: How did the redneck find his sister in the forest?
A: Not bad.

Q: How do you circumcise a redneck?
A: Kick his sister in the jaw.

Q: What do you call a redneck virgin?
A: A girl who can run faster than her daddy.

Q: What does a redneck girl say when she loses her virginity?
A: "Gramps, you're crushin' my smokes."

Q: Why do redneck schools only have Drivers' Ed two days a week?
A: Because they need their cars for Sex Ed the other three days a week.

A redneck took his daughter to the gynecologist. The doctor asked, "So what are you here for today?"

The father answered, "To get my daughter on birth control."

"Is your daughter sexually active?" the doctor asked.

"No sir," answered the redneck. "She just lies there like her mother."

Yo mama's so fat . . .

Her nickname is "Damn!"

When you get on top of her your ears pop.

She needs a hula hoop to keep her socks up.

When she goes to a restaurant she doesn't get a menu, she gets an estimate.

She took a spoon to the Super Bowl.

She sat on four quarters and made a dollar.

She has more rolls than a bakery.

She sat on a rainbow and got Skittles.

The last time she saw *90210* was on a scale.

She sat on a scale, and it said, "To be continued."

Yo mama's so ugly . . .

They filmed *Gorillas in the Mist* in her shower.

She makes blind people go lame.

She looks like her face caught on fire and they put it out with a fork.

She didn't get hit with the ugly stick, she got hit with the ugly log.

When she entered an ugly contest they said, "Sorry, no professionals."

She looks like she's been in a dryer filled with rocks.

When your dad wants to have sex in the car, he tells her to get out.

She looks like she got hit with a bag of "What the fuck?!"

Q: Why do so many white people get lost skiing?
A: It's hard to find them in the snow.

Q: Why did God invent golf?
A: So white people could dress up like blacks.

Q: How do you stop four white guys from raping a white woman?
A: Throw them a golf ball.

Q: What does a bird have that white girls don't?
A: Breasts.

Q: What's the flattest surface on the planet?
A: A white girl's ass.

Q: How many white girls does it take to screw in a light bulb?
A: None. White girls can't screw.

Q: How many white men does it take to screw in a light bulb?
A: One. White men will screw anything.

Q: What did the black guy do with his M&Ms?
A: He ate them.

Q: What did the white guy do with his M&Ms?
A: He put them in alphabetical order.

Q: What's twelve inches long, hard, and white?
A: Nothing. It only comes in black.

Q: What does a white man do at the nightclub?
A: Cry while all the colored folk are bumpin' and grindin' with his fine white bitches.

Q: What do you call a white person on fire?
A: A fire cracker.

Q: Why shouldn't white people go swimming?
A: Because crackers get soggy when wet.

Q: What do you call a black man in a sleeping bag?
A: Snickers.

Q: What do you call two black men in a sleeping bag?
A: Twix.

Q: Why are black men's eyes always red after sex?
A: From the mace.

Q: What do you call a black man and a white woman in a sleeping bag?
A: Rape.

Q: Why did God give black men large penises?
A: As a way of saying "Sorry" for putting pubic hair on their heads.

Q: What did God say when the second black person was born?
A: Damn. I burned another one.

Q: How do you drown a black person?
A: Pop their lips.

Q: What does a black woman get when she has an abortion?
A: A thank-you letter from the welfare office and a five-hundred-dollar gift certificate from Crime Stoppers.

Q: What are the best ten years of a black kid's life?
A: Third grade.

Q: What's the difference between a black man and a park bench?
A: A park bench can support a family of four.

Q: Why are black people so fast?
A: Because all the slow ones are in jail.

Q: How do you get a black kid to stop jumping on the bed?
A: Put Velcro on the ceiling.

Q: How do you get him down?
A: Yell "Piñata!" at the Mexican kids next door.

Q: What's the difference between a black man and a bicycle?
A: A bicycle doesn't sing when you put chains on it.

Q: Why do you throw a rock at a black guy on a bike?
A: To get your slave back.

Q: What do black kids get for Christmas?
A: Your bike.

Q: What do you call a black man flying an airplane?
A: The pilot, you racist.

Q: What do you say to a black Jew?
A: Get in the back of the oven.

Q: Why do Mexican kids eat tamales on Christmas?
A: So they have something to unwrap.

Q: How many cops does it take to arrest a Mexican?
A: Two. One to arrest him and the other to hold his oranges.

Q: Why do you throw a rock at a Mexican on a bike?
A: To get your bike back.

Q: Why don't Mexicans cross the border in groups of three?
A: Because it says "No Trespassing."

Q: What do you call five Mexicans on the bottom of a pool?
A: Sinko.

Q: What was the last thing Jesus said to the Mexicans?
A: "Don't do anything until I get back!"

Q: Why aren't there any Mexicans on *Star Trek*?
A: They won't work in the future, either.

Q: What do you call two Mexicans playing basketball?
A: Juan on Juan.

Q: What do you call a group of stoned Mexicans?
A: Baked beans.

Q: What do you call a skinny Mexican?
A: A chicostick.

Q: What do you call a Mexican crossed with an octopus?
A: Who knows, but you should see it pick lettuce!

Q: What do you call a Mexican baptism?
A: Bean dip.

Q: What do you call a midget Mexican?
A: Paragraph. Because he's too short to be an essay.

Q: When does a Mexican become Spanish?
A: When he marries your daughter.

6

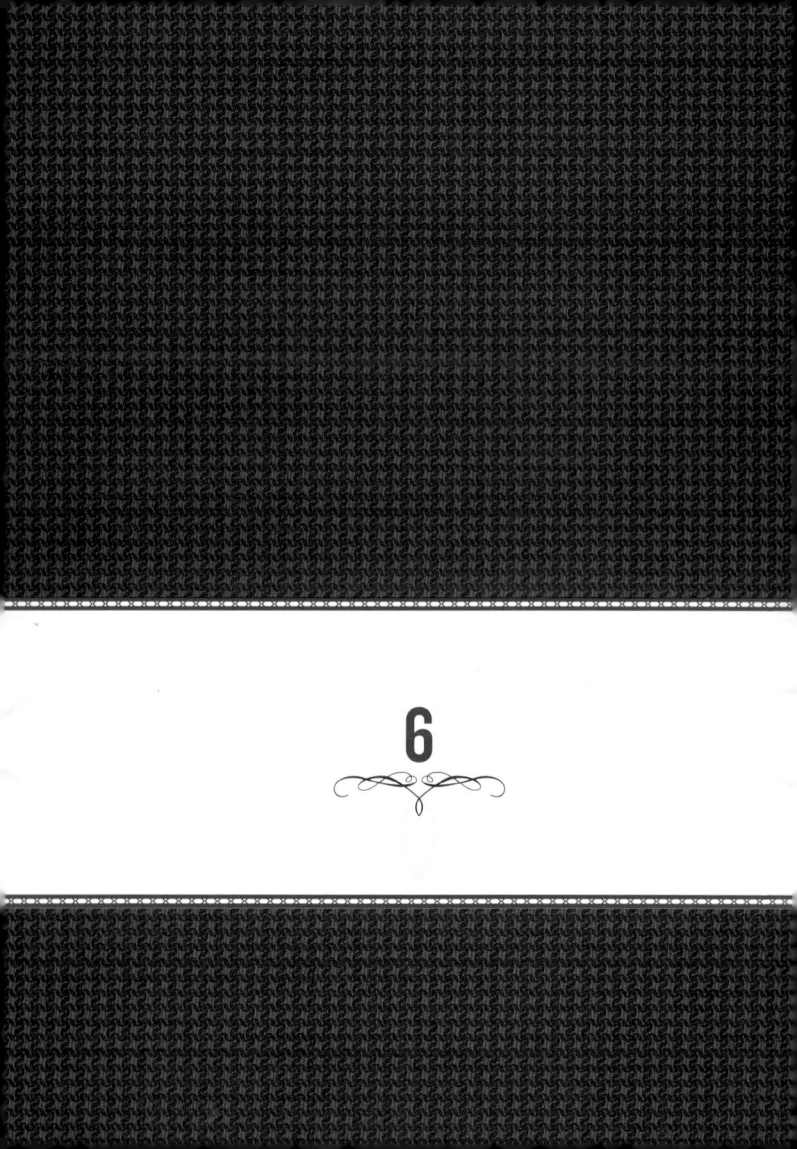

RUDE RELATIONSHIPS

THE PSYCHOANALYST ERICH FROMM FAMOUSLY WROTE, "LOVE IS THE ONLY SANE AND SATISFACTORY ANSWER TO THE PROBLEM OF HUMAN EXISTENCE." CLEARLY, THE TORMENTED CHARACTERS IN THIS CHAPTER WOULD BENEFIT FROM AN HOUR ON ERICH FROMM'S COUCH.

The truth is that where there is love, there is pain. The pain of unrequited love and the pain of watching your true love grow old, fat, and farty. The pain of heartbreak and the pain of discovering your wife having sex with the pool man. The pain of separation and the pain of breaking a nail while holding the pillow over your ex-husband's face.

Q: Why is it so hard for women to find men who are sensitive, caring, and good-looking?
A: Because those men already have boyfriends.

Q: How many honest, intelligent, and caring men in the world does it take to do the dishes?
A: Both of them.

Q: What's the difference between a singles bar and a circus?
A: At a circus, the clowns don't talk.

Q: How are men and parking spots alike?
A: The good ones are always taken and the ones that are left are handicapped.

Q: How does a man plan for his future?
A: He buys two cases of beer, instead of one.

Q: What did God say after he created man?
A: I can do way better than this.

Q: How do you know God is a man?
A: If God were a woman, semen would taste like chocolate.

Q: What do a clitoris, an anniversary, and a toilet have in common?
A: Men always miss them.

Q: Why do men want to marry virgins?
A: Because they can't stand criticism.

Q: Why do men find it difficult to make eye contact?
A: Because breasts don't have eyes.

Q: Why did God invent orgasms?
A: So men would know when to stop fucking.

A man walks into a flower shop and says, "I need some flowers."

"Of course," the florist says, "what do you have in mind?"

"I'm not really sure."

The florist says, "Let me ask that a different way. What exactly have you done?"

Q: What does it mean when a man is in your bed gasping for breath and calling your name?
A: You didn't hold the pillow down long enough.

Q: Why are almost all serial killers men?
A: Because women prefer to kill one man slowly over many, many years.

Q: Why did God create man?
A: Because a vibrator can't mow the lawn.

Q: How can you tell if a man is sexually excited?
A: He's breathing.

Q: Why do men name their penises?
A: They want to be on a first-name basis with the person who makes all the decisions.

Q: Why do penises have holes in the ends?
A: So men can be open-minded.

Q: What do men and sperm have in common?
A: They both have a 1 in 10 million chance of becoming human.

Q: How many men does it take to screw a light bulb?
A: Five. One to do the screwing, and four to listen to him brag.

Q: What happens to men who mix Viagra and Prozac?
A: They're ready to go, but not sure where.

Q: Why is a theme park like Viagra?
A: In both cases you wait three hours for a two-minute ride.

Q: Why is sleeping with a man like a soap opera?
A: Just when it starts to get interesting, it's over until next week.

Q: What do you call pulling off a woman's panty hose?
A: Foreplay.

Q: Why don't women blink during foreplay?
A: They don't have time.

Q: Why do women have vaginas?
A: So men will talk to them.

Q: Why do women have foreheads?
A: So you have somewhere to kiss after getting a blow job.

Q: Why is the space between a woman's breasts and her hips called a waist?
A: Because you could easily fit another pair of tits there.

Q: What do you say to a woman with no arms and no legs?
A: Nice tits.

Q: How do you make five pounds of fat look good?
A: Put a nipple on it.

Q: What are the small bumps around a woman's nipples for?
A: It's Braille for "suck here."

Q: Why did God invent alcohol?
A: So ugly girls can have sex, too.

Q: What does an ugly girl put behind her ears to attract men?
A: Her ankles.

Dave and Greg are talking about Freudian slips and how embarrassing they can be. Greg recalls the time he was at the airport with his wife, buying plane tickets to Pittsburgh, and mistakenly asked the large-chested blonde behind the counter for "two pickets to Tittsburgh."

They chuckle, and Dave shares his own story. "We were sitting at the dinner table, and I meant to ask my wife to pass the butter. But instead I said, 'Thanks for ruining my life, you fucking bitch.'"

Q: Why did God create women?
A: Because sheep are lousy cooks.

Q: What's the difference between a woman and a battery?
A: Batteries have a positive side.

Q: Why do they call it a Pap smear?
A: Because nobody wants a cunt scrape.

Top Five Worst First-Date Movies

Relationships are hard. Do not make things harder by watching any of the following movies on a first date.

1. SEX, LIES, AND VIDEOTAPE (1989)
Imdb.com nails this one! Here's their description: "A sexually repressed woman's husband is having an affair with her sister. The arrival of a visitor with a rather unusual fetish changes everything."

2. WAITRESS (2007)
A pregnant waitress trying to turn around her life has an evil husband who steals her paychecks and wants to film homemade sex tapes after the baby is born. Spoiler alert: This does not end well.

3. THE BREAK-UP (2006)

Vince Vaughn and Jennifer Aniston are breaking up and each is trying hard to keep their fancy condo from falling into the other's hands. They decide to live together as "roommates"—that is, roommates who play strip poker and date other people in order to provoke each other. It's 106 minutes of unhappy people acting nasty.

4. (500) DAYS OF SUMMER (2009)

You can sum this movie up in six words: She's just not that into you. It's a real bummer, too, since we're talking about Zooey Deschanel here.

5. DATE NIGHT (2010)

Somehow a movie starring Tina Fey and Steve Carell is unfunny—and unromantic. It's the ultimate first-date downer.

Q: Why did God invent yeast infections?
A: So women know what it feels like to live with an annoying cunt.

Q: Why did cavemen drag their women around by the hair?
A: Because if you drag them around by the feet, they fill up with dirt.

Q: Why do women wear makeup and perfume?
A: Because they're ugly and they smell bad.

Q: Why do women pierce their belly button?
A: Place to hang their air freshener.

A man walks up to a woman in a bar and says, "Do you want to dance?"

The woman looks him over and says, "I don't really like this song. Even if I did, I wouldn't dance with you."

The man says, "I'm so sorry, you must have misunderstood me. I said, 'You look fat in those pants.'"

Q: What's the best thing about contraceptive sponges?
A: After sex, women can wash the dishes.

Q: Why did the woman cross the road?
A: Never mind that, what the hell is she doing out of the kitchen?

Q: What's the difference between a woman and a cat?
A: One is a finicky eater who doesn't care if you live or die. The other is a house pet.

Q: How many feminists does it take to change a light bulb?
A: Two. One to change the bulb and one to suck my dick.

Q: Why do women close their eyes during sex?
A: They can't stand to see a man having a good time.

Q: What's the definition of eternity?
A: The time between when you cum and when she leaves.

Q: Did you hear about the guy who finally figured out women?
A: He died laughing before he could tell anybody.

A man is visiting his friend's house and sees a rubber object on the coffee table, so he asks his friend, "What's this?"

"It's an artificial vagina," his friend says. "And it's the best fuck I have ever had!"

"You gotta be kidding," the first man says. "A fake vagina is your best fuck ever?"

"OK, you don't believe me? Why don't you take it home and give it a try?"

So his friend takes the fake vagina home, tries it out, and discovers that it's true–it is the best sex of his entire life. Later that day, the man's wife walks into the kitchen and sees the rubber object on the table.

"What's this?" she asks.

"It's an artificial vagina, and it's the best fuck I've ever had in my entire life," replies the husband.

"If it's so good," asks the wife, "then what's it doing in the kitchen?"

"Well," says the husband, "as soon as I can teach it to cook, you are outta here."

Q: What's the longest sentence in the English language?
A: I do.

Q: Why are wedding dresses white?
A: Aren't all kitchen appliances?

Q: What's the definition of divorce?
A: The future tense of marriage.

Q: If first marriages are triumphs of imagination over intelligence, what are second marriages?
A: Triumphs of hope over experience.

Q: What is the only thing divorce proves?
A: Whose mother was right in the first place.

Q: Why are divorces so expensive?
A: Because they're worth it.

Q: Did you hear about the new "Divorce Barbie"?
A: It comes with all of Ken's stuff.

A man is discussing his upcoming wedding with a friend. "I'm only worried about one thing: I'm not sure if my future bride is a virgin or not."

His friend replies, "Oh, there's an easy test for that. All you need is some red paint, some blue paint, and a shovel. On your wedding day you simply paint one of your balls red and one blue. That night if she laughs and says, 'Those are the funniest balls I've ever seen!' you hit her with the shovel."

7

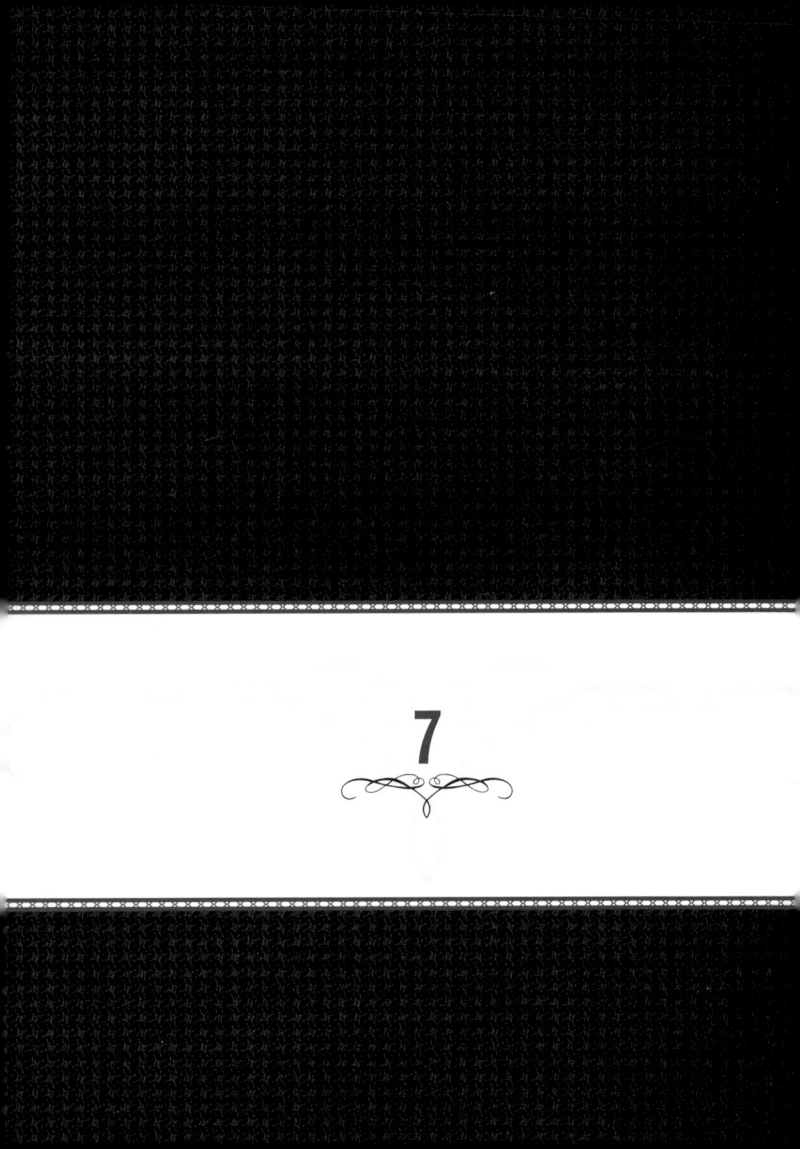

RUDE SEX

BLOW JOB! PENIS! LESBIANS! LET'S NOT MINCE WORDS. THIS CHAPTER'S THEME IS SEX—BE IT STRAIGHT, GAY, KINKY, OR OTHERWISE.

A man and a woman meet in a bar and hit it off. Later they go back to her place. While taking off his clothes, the guy notices three shelves above the woman's bed, each packed with teddy bears. Little bears are lined up on the bottom shelf, medium-sized bears on the middle shelf, large bears on the top shelf.

After fifteen minutes of grunting and groaning, the guy lies back and asks, "So, how was that?"

The woman replies, "You can choose any bear from the bottom shelf."

Q: What is it when a man talks dirty to a woman?
A: Sexual harassment.

Q: What is it when a woman talks dirty to a man?
A: $4.99 a minute.

Q: What's the speed limit of sex?
A: Sixty-eight. Because at 69 you have to turn around.

Q: What's the square root of 69?
A: Ate something.

Q: What's the square root of 6.9?
A: A good thing screwed up by a period.

Q: What is 69 + 69?
A: Dinner for four.

Q: What's the difference between 69 and a family reunion?
A: In 69 you only have to kiss one dick.

Q: What comes after 69?
A: Mouthwash.

Q: What is 71?
A: 69 with two fingers up your ass.

Q: What is 34½?
A: 69 for midgets.

Q: What is 68?
A: You blow me, I'll owe you one.

A young boy asks his mom, "Mommy, where do babies come from?"

"From storks," she replies sheepishly.

"I know that," the boy says, "but who fucks the storks?"

Q: What's the difference between erotic and kinky?
A: Erotic is using a feather. Kinky is using the whole chicken.

Q: What's the difference between "Oooh!" and "Aaah!"?
A: About three inches.

Q: What's the difference between light and hard?
A: You can sleep with a light on.

Q: What do a Rubik's Cube and a penis have in common?
A: The more you play with them, the harder they get.

"You know that beautiful girl at work I wanted to ask out?" a guy asks his friend.

"You mean the girl who gives you an erection every time you see her?" the friend replies.

"Yeah, that's the one. I finally worked up the courage to ask her out, and she agreed."

"That's great!" says the friend. "So what's the problem?"

"I went to meet her last night, but I was worried I'd get an erection again. So I got some duct tape and taped my penis to my leg. That way, if I got an erection it wouldn't show."

"Sensible," the friend says. "Then what happened?"

"So I get to her house and ring the doorbell. She answers wearing the sexiest dress you ever saw."

"And then what happened?"

"I kicked her in the face."

Q: What's better than a rose on your piano?
A: Tulips on your organ.

Q: What is better than a cold Bud?
A: A warm bush.

Q: What's the definition of a Yankee?
A: Same thing as a "quickie" only you do it yourself.

A woman walks past her daughter's closed bedroom door and hears a strange buzzing noise coming from within. Opening the door, she finds her daughter masturbating with a vibrator. Somewhat shocked, she asks, "What in the world are you doing?"

The daughter replies, "Mom, I'm thirty-six years old, unmarried, and this thing is about as close as I'll ever get to a husband. Please, go away and leave me alone!"

The next day, the girl's father hears the same buzz coming from the other side of the closed bedroom door. Opening the door, he also finds his daughter masturbating with a vibrator. "Dad," the daughter explains, "I'm thirty-six years old, unmarried, and this thing is about as close as I'll ever get to a husband. Please, go away and leave me alone!"

A few days later, mom and daughter come home from a shopping trip and hear a strange buzzing noise coming from the living room. They walk in together and find the girl's father sitting on the couch, staring at the TV. The vibrator is next to him on the couch, buzzing like crazy.

"What the hell are you doing?" the wife asks.

"I'm watching the ball game with my son-in-law," he replies.

Fifty Ways to Say "Penis"

Does your man-junk need a new dickname? Here are fifty popular penile sobriquets to try on for size.

1. baby maker
2. big fella
3. bologna pony
4. boner
5. cack
6. Captain Winky
7. choad
8. chub
9. cock
10. dick
11. ding-a-ling
12. ding-dong
13. dong
14. hard-on
15. jimmy
16. johnson
17. knob
18. long dong
19. love muscle
20. love shaft
21. love stick
22. meat popsicle
23. member
24. one-eyed monster
25. one-eyed willy
26. package
27. pecker
28. percy
29. peter
30. piece
31. pipe cleaner
32. plonker
33. pork sword
34. prick
35. pud
36. rod
37. salami
38. sausage
39. schlong
40. shaft
41. stiffy
42. tool
43. trouser snake
44. tube steak
45. wang
46. wang thang
47. wee wee
48. weenie
49. wiener
50. wily

Q: What's the difference between love, true love, and showing off?
A: Spit, swallow, and gargle.

Q: Why do men pay more for car insurance?
A: Women don't get blow jobs while they're driving.

Q: What's the difference between a blimp and 365 blow jobs?
A: One is a good year, the other is a great year.

Two sperms are racing to impregnate an egg. "Hey, how much longer until we reach the ovaries?" one sperm asks the other.

"Keep swimming," the second sperm replies. "We haven't even passed the tonsils yet."

Q: How do you know your girlfriend is too young for you?
A: You have to make airplane noises to get your penis in her mouth.

Q: How can you tell you have a high sperm count?
A: Your girlfriend must chew before she can swallow.

Q: What do a tightrope walker and a man getting a blow job from a sixty-five-year-old woman have in common?
A: In both cases it's unsafe to look down.

A young boy was taking a Sex Ed class. The teacher drew a penis on the chalkboard and asked, "Does anybody know what this is?"

The boy answered, "Of course, I do. My dad has two of them."

"Two?" the teacher asked with arched eyebrows.

"Yeah, two," the boy replied, "a small one for peeing and a big one for brushing the babysitter's teeth."

Q: What's the most intelligent thing to come out of a woman's mouth?
A: Einstein's cock.

Q: What's the difference between your paycheck and your cock?
A: You don't have to beg your girlfriend to blow your paycheck.

Q: What's the difference between your wife and your job?
A: After five years your job will still suck.

Q: Which doesn't belong: wife, eggs, or blow job?
A: Blow job. You can beat your wife, you can beat your eggs, but you can't beat a blow job.

Q: Why is chocolate better than a blow job?
A: Chocolate satisfies even when it's gone soft.

Q: Why is chocolate better than a blow job?
A: You can have chocolate while driving.

Q: Why is chocolate better than a blow job?
A: If you bite the nuts too hard, the chocolate doesn't mind.

A man and wife are in tough financial straits, they're broke and they need money. So they decide the wife will become a hooker. She's not quite sure what to do, so her husband says, "Stand in front of that bar and pick up any well-dressed guy who walks out. Tell him you charge a hundred bucks. If you got a question, I'll be parked around the corner."

After a few minutes a well-dressed man walks out of the bar and she smiles suggestively. He asks, "How much?"

She says, "A hundred dollars."

He says, "All I got is forty bucks on me."

She says, "Hang on!" and runs around the corner to her husband. "What should I offer for forty bucks?"

"A hand job," the husband replies.

She runs back and tells the guy all he gets for forty dollars is a hand job. He agrees. She gets in the car. He unzips his pants and exposes a rather large penis. She stares at it for a minute, and then says, "I'll be right back."

She runs back to her husband and asks, "Can you loan this guy sixty bucks?"

Q: What's the difference between sin and shame?
A: It's a sin to put it in. It's a shame to pull it out.

Q: What's the difference between a woman and a coffin?
A: You come in one and go in the other.

Q: What did the depressed penis say to the psychiatrist?
A: "Doc, I'm surrounded by nuts and my neighbor's an asshole."

Q: What happens if you take Viagra and Rogaine at the same time?
A: You have a stiff, hairy penis.

Q: What did the penis say to the condom?
A: "Cover me, I'm going in."

Q: Why do midgets laugh when they run?
A: Because the grass tickles their balls.

Q: What is the difference between snowmen and snow-women?
A: Snowballs.

Little Red Riding Hood was walking through the woods. Suddenly the Big Bad Wolf jumped from behind a tree and said, "Little Red Riding Hood, I'm going to screw your brains out."

Little Red Riding Hood calmly reached into her picnic basket and pulled out a gun and aimed it at the wolf. "No you're not," she said. "You're going to eat me, just like it says in the book."

Q: What is the definition of a perfect lover?
A: A man with an eight-inch tongue who can breathe through his ears.

Q: What's the definition of female masturbation?
A: Finishing the job off properly.

Q: How do you know God meant for men to eat pussy?
A: Why else would he make it look like a taco.

Q: What did the banana say to the vibrator?
A: "Why are you shaking? I'm the one she's gonna eat."

Q: What do you call a truck full of dildos?
A: Toys for Twats.

Q: What's the difference between a slut and a bitch?
A: A slut sleeps with everyone. A bitch sleeps with everyone but you.

A man walks into a bar and orders a beer. The barmaid is extremely attractive, and he asks, "Can I buy you a drink?"

The barmaid says, "You've no chance with me, love. I'm a lesbian."

"What's a lesbian?" the man asks.

"You see that blonde at the end of the bar, the one with the big tits?" the barmaid says. "Well, I want to rip off her shirt and suck her nipples."

"Holy shit!" the man says, "I must be a lesbian, too!"

Q: What did one lesbian say to another?
A: "Your face or mine?"

Q: What's the new and politically correct name for lesbian?
A: Vagitarian.

Q: What do you call a lesbian Eskimo?
A: Klondike.

Q: What do you call a lesbian with fat fingers?
A: Well hung.

Q: How many lesbians does it take to screw in a light bulb?
A: Four. One to change it, two to organize the potluck, and one to write a folk song about the empowering experience.

Q: What do you call one thousand armed lesbians?
A: Militia Etheridge.

Q: What do you call a one-hundred-pound lesbian?
A: Weed whacker.

Q: What do you call a three-hundred-pound lesbian?
A: Bush hog.

Thirty Ways to Say "Vagina"

1.	ax wound	16.	hoo-ha
2.	bearded clam	17.	meat curtains
3.	beaver	18.	minge
4.	box	19.	moneymaker
5.	bush	20.	muff
6.	cigar box	21.	pink sink
7.	cock pocket	22.	pink taco
8.	cockpit	23.	poon
9.	cooch	24.	poontang
10.	coochie	25.	pussy
11.	cunt	26.	quim
12.	fanny	27.	snatch
13.	fuck hole	28.	twat
14.	hair pie	29.	va-jai-jai
15.	hole	30.	yoni

Haven't heard the song "Love Your Vagina" by Amanda Dawson? It's a catchy little advertising jingle for a tampon-replacement product called the Mooncup (www.loveyourvagina.com), featuring hundreds more popular pudenda pet names.

Q: What do you call lesbian twins?
A: Lick-a-likes.

Q: How can you tell you're in a lesbian bar?
A: Even the pool table has no balls.

Q: What is the leading cause in death with lesbians?
A: Hairballs.

Q: What do you call a lesbian dinosaur?
A: Lickalotopuss.

Q: What do you call a gay dinosaur?
A: Megasaurass.

Q: How do you know if your best friend is gay?
A: He gets a hard-on when you're fucking him up the ass.

Q: What is the difference between oral sex and anal sex?
A: Oral sex makes your day. Anal sex makes your hole weak.

Q: What's the first symptom of AIDS?
A: A sharp, stabbing pain in your ass.

Q: What did the first condom say to the second condom as they walked past the gay bar?
A: "Wanna go get shit-faced?"

Q: Why did the condom fly across the room?
A: Because it was pissed off.

Q: What's the difference between a gay man and a refrigerator?
A: The refrigerator doesn't fart when you pull the meat out.

Q: What did the gay couple say when, all of a sudden, a condom floated to the surface in the hot tub?
A: "Who farted?"

Q: How do you clean a condom?
A: Hold it between your fingers and shake the fuck out of it.

Q: What do gays and ambulances have in common?
A: They both get loaded from the rear and go "Woo hoo!"

Q: How many gay men does it take to change a light bulb?
A: Two. One to change it and one to say, "Fabulous."

Q: Is it better to be born black or gay?
A: Black, because you don't have to tell your parents.

A woman and her fetus walk into a clinic. "I'm scared," the fetus says.

"How do you think I feel?" the woman replies. "I have to walk out of here alone."

Q: What do you call a man at an abortion clinic?
A: Relieved.

Q: Why can't you fool an aborted fetus?
A: Because it wasn't born yesterday.

Q: What's the difference between a television and my pregnant girlfriend?
A: When I put a coat hanger inside my pregnant girlfriend, I didn't get a very good reception.

Q: Why did the fetus cross the road?
A: Because they moved the Dumpster.

Two old men go to a brothel. The madam asks what they'd most like to experience. "Well, ma'am, we'd both like to spend the evening with a woman."

"How old are you, gentlemen?"

One of the men replies, "We're twin brothers, born the same day, and we just turned ninety-five."

The madam tells one of the working girls to take the brothers upstairs and put each of them in a room with a blow-up doll. So the men go upstairs and do their thing. When they come back downstairs one of the brothers asks the other, "So how was it?"

"Not so good," his brother replied. "I think the girl was dead. She just lay there. How was yours?"

"I think mine was a witch," the brother replied.

"A witch??"

"Yeah. I bit her on the tit and she farted. Then she flew out the window."

Q: Know what the leper said to the prostitute?
A: Keep the tip.

Q: Who makes more money, a drug dealer or a hooker?
A: A hooker, because she can wash her crack and reuse it.

Q: What do bungee jumping and hookers have in common?
A: They both cost a hundred bucks and if the rubber breaks, you're screwed.

Q: What's the difference between an epileptic oyster fisherman, and a hooker with diarrhea?
A: One of them shucks between fits.

Q: What did the doctor say to the hooker who complained no hair would grow on her vagina?
A: "Did you ever see grass grow on a highway?"

Q: If a young hooker uses Vaseline, what does an old hooker use?
A: Poligrip.

Q: What do you call a Serbian prostitute?
A: Sloberdown Mycockyoubitch.

Q: What do you call a hooker with no legs?
A: A nightcrawler.

Q: What do you tell a hooker with two black eyes?
A: Nothing. You've already told her twice.

Q: What does a homeless hooker use for a vibrator?
A: Two flies in a bottle.

Classic Dead Hooker Jokes

Q: How many cops does it take to push a hooker down the stairs?
A: None. She fell.

Q: What's the difference between your job and a dead hooker?
A: Your job still sucks.

Q: Why did the hooker fall out of the tree?
A: Because she was dead.

Q: What's the difference between Jell-O and a dead hooker?
A: Jell-O wiggles when you eat it.

Q: What's the difference between a Corvette and a dead hooker?
A: I don't have a Corvette in my garage.

Q: What do you do if your hooker is screaming and bleeding in your hotel room?
A: Shoot her again.

Q: What's the difference between an onion and a hooker?
A: You don't cry when you chop up a hooker.

A prostitute went to the doctor complaining of morning sickness. The doctor says, "Congratulations, you're pregnant! Do you know who the father is?"

"Doc," the prostitute replied, "if you ate a can of beans, would you know which one made you fart?"

8

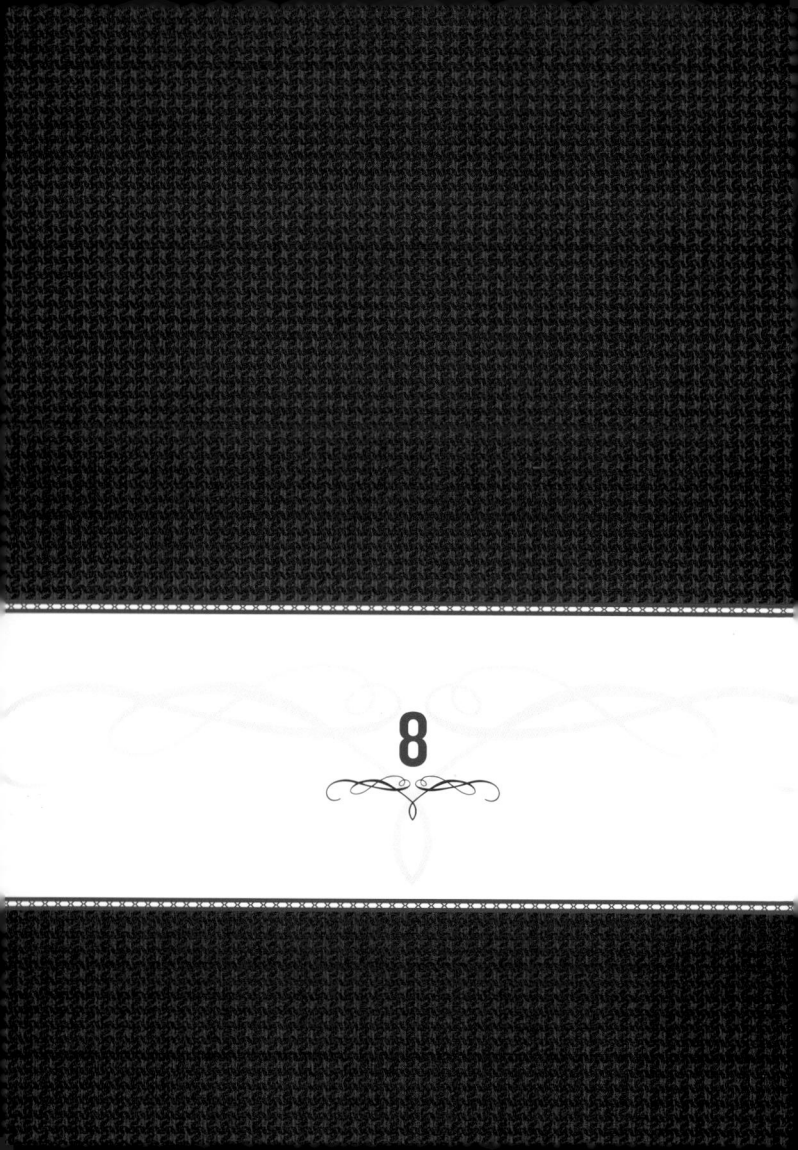

SICK & TWISTED

VERY FEW BOOKS ARE BLESSED WITH MICHAEL JACKSON, DEAD BABIES, AND BALL-LICKING DOGS IN THE SAME CHAPTER. THINK OF THIS CHAPTER AS A FRAGRANT POTPOURRI OF THE OFFENSIVE, CRUDE, AND CRASS.

A man goes into a library and asks for a book on suicide. The librarian says, "Fuck off, you won't bring it back."

Q: What's worse than being depressed?
A: Nothing. But it's no worse than anything else since life sucks anyway.

Q: What's worse than being dead?
A: Being alive and depressed.

Q: How many psychiatrists does it take to change a light bulb?
A: None. The light bulb will change itself, when it's ready.

Q: How many psychiatrists does it take to change a light bulb?
A: How long have you been having this fantasy?

Q: How many psychiatrists does it take to change a light bulb?
A: How many do you think it takes?

A: One.
Q: How many clairvoyants does it take to change a light bulb?

Q: What did the battery say to the gynecologist?
A: It's not the smell that bothers me, it's the discharge.

Q: What do gynecologists and pizza boys have in common?
A: They can smell it, but they can't eat it.

An old lady goes to the dentist and, after sitting in the examination chair, lowers her underwear and raises her legs. The dentist says, "Excuse me, but I'm not a gynecologist."

"I know," replies the old lady. "I want you to take my husband's teeth out."

Q: What did the nurse say when she found a rectal thermometer in her pocket?
A: "Some asshole has my pen."

Q: What's the difference between an oral thermometer and a rectal thermometer?
A: The taste.

Q: What's the biggest problem working in a paperless office?
A: Needing to shit.

Q: What's eight inches long and starts with a *P*?
A: A turd.

A little boy with diarrhea tells his mom that he needs Viagra. The surprised mom asks, "Why do you need that?"

The little boy replies, "Isn't that what you give dad when his shit doesn't get hard?"

Q: What's the definition of surprise?
A: A fart with a lump in it.

Q: What's the definition of bravery?
A: A man with diarrhea, chancing a fart.

Q: What's the definition of a wet fart?
A: A turd honking for the right of way.

The teacher asks little Johnny to use the word "definitely" in a sentence. Little Johnny replies, "Teacher, do farts have lumps in them?"

The teacher replies, "Of course not, Johnny."

To which Johnny replies, "Then I have definitely shit my pants."

Two guys are in a locker room when one notices the other has a cork stuck up his ass. He asks, "How'd you get a cork stuck in your ass?"

The other guy replies, "I was walking along the beach and tripped over a lamp. There was a puff of smoke, and then a genie in a turban popped out. He said, 'I am the genie of the lamp, I can grant you one wish.'

"And I said, 'No shit.'"

A Short History of the Word Shit

In the early Internet days, an urban legend credited the word *shit* to nineteenth-century sailors who loaded manure into boats and—in the interest of making a long and unfunny story much shorter—discovered the hard way that manure and seawater produce methane gas, which is explosive. A few dead seamen later, manure loaders started labeling their ships S.H.I.T., an acronym for "ship high in transit," referring to the fact that manure should be stored on higher decks to avoid contamination with seawater.

Or so the urban legend goes.

The truth is that "shit" has been around a long time, showing up in written works as both a noun and a verb as far back as the fourteenth century. It's a derivative of the Old English words *scite* and *scitte* (meaning "dung" and "diarrhea," respectively), and the Indo-European root *skei-*, meaning "to cut" (so it's distantly related to modern words such as *schism* and *science*). For most of history, "shit" was spelled "shite" (and is still pronounced with a long *i* in parts of Ireland and the United Kingdom). The shortened four-letter version made its first written appearance in the late 1700s.

Can't get enough of shit? Add *History of Shit* to your reading list. The book is by Dominique Laporte, a post-Marxist French psychoanalyst who died at age thirty-five in 1984 (just think of the many fascinating tomes denied the world by Laporte's early death). His main argument here is that the management of human waste is the driving force behind both our identities as modern individuals and the development of capitalism. (If you think about it, the man has a point.)

A man is walking his dog through the graveyard when he sees another man crouching behind a gravestone.

"Morning," he says.

"No," the other man replies. "Just having a shit."

Q: Why do dogs lick their own balls?
A: To get the taste of dog food out of their mouths.

Q: Why do dogs lick their own balls?
A: Because dogs can't make a fist.

Q: Why do dogs lick their own balls?
A: Because they know in a minute they're going to lick your face.

Q: How do you get a dog to stop humping your leg?
A: Lick its balls.

A little boy asks his dad, "Daddy, is God a man or a woman?"

"Both, son; God is both."

A few minutes later the little boy asks his dad, "Daddy, is God black or white?"

"Both, son; both," the dad replies.

"Daddy, does God love children?"

"Yes, son, he loves all children."

A few minutes later the little boy asks, "Daddy, is Michael Jackson God?"

Q: What's the difference between Michael Jackson and a plastic bag?
A: One is white, plastic, and dangerous to young children. The other is a plastic bag.

Q: How does Michael Jackson know it's time for bed?
A: When the big hand is on the little hand.

Q: Why did Michael Jackson place a phone call to Boyz II Men?
A: He thought it was a delivery service.

Q: What's the worst stain to try and remove from little boy's pants?
A: Michael Jackson's makeup.

Q: What's Michael Jackson's favorite nursery rhyme?
A: Little Boy Blew.

Q: What's the difference between Michael Jackson and acne?
A: Acne doesn't come on your face until you're thirteen.

Q: Why did Michael Jackson get food poisoning?
A: He ate twelve-year-old nuts.

Q: What do Michael Jackson and Michael Jordan have in common?
A: They both played ball in the minor leagues.

Q: Why did Michael Jackson not like eating at Taco Bell?
A: Because he didn't like thinking outside the bun.

A boy asked his father, "Dad, what's the difference between potentially and realistically?"

The father thought for a moment and answered, "Go ask your mother if she would sleep with Brad Pitt for a million bucks. Then ask your sister and brother if they'd each sleep with Brad Pitt for a million bucks. Come back and tell me what you've learned."

So the boy asked his mother, "Mom, would you sleep with Brad Pitt for a million bucks?"

His mother replied, "Of course! We could really use the money to fix up the house and pay for your education."

The boy asked his sister the same question, and she answered, "Oh my God! Oh my God! I love Brad Pitt. I'd sleep with him in a second. The million bucks is just icing on the beefcake."

The boy then asked his brother, who replied, "Of course I would, you dumbass. I could really use the money."

The next day the boy's father asked, "So did you find out the difference between potentially and realistically?"

"Yes, I did," the boy answered. "Potentially, you and I are sitting on three million bucks, but realistically, we're living with two hookers and a homo."

Q: What's the worst thing about screwing a three-year-old?
A: Getting blood on your clown suit.

Q: What's the best thing about having sex with a five-year-old?
A: Getting to beat them to death in the woods afterward.

Q: What's the best thing about having sex with a six-year-old girl?
A: Pretending she's a six-year-old boy.

Q: What's the best thing about having sex with little boys?
A: Their small hands make your penis look big.

Q: What's the best thing about having sex with a six-year-old boy?
A: Not having to pretend!

A little girl comes home from school with a smile on her face, and tells her mother, "A boy at school showed me his penis on the playground today."

Before the mother can say anything the little girl adds, "It reminded me of a peanut."

"It was really small, was it?" the mom asks.

"No," the little girl replies, "it was salty."

A guy walks into a bar and sees his best friend. "You won't believe what just happened. I was taking a shortcut along the train tracks and I found a girl tied to the rails. I untied her, and then we had sex over and over again."

"That's amazing," his friend says. "Did you get a blow job, too?"

"No," his friend replies, "I never found her head."

Q: What kind of file do you need to turn a one-inch hole into a six-inch hole?
A: Pedophile.

Q: What's a pedophile's favorite part of a hockey game?
A: The first period.

Q: What's black and blue and afraid of sex?
A: The six-year-old in my basement.

Q: Why is there no such thing as bestial necrophilia?
A: Because you'd just be flogging a dead horse.

A pedophile pulls up in his car beside a little boy. Holding a bag full of candy, he says, "Hey kid, if I give you a piece of candy, will you come in my car?"

"Hell, mister," the little boy replies. "Give me the whole bag and I'll come in your mouth!"

Q: What's the difference between a horse carriage and a miscarriage?
A: You can't eat a horse carriage.

Q: What's red and follows behind a train?
A: A miscarriage.

Q: What is green, lies in a ditch, and smells like shit?
A: A dead Girl Scout.

Q: What's blue and sticky?
A: Smurf cum.

Q: What's gray and comes in pints?
A: An elephant.

Q: What's black and white and red all over?
A: Panda rape.

Q: What's blue and doesn't fit?
A: A dead epileptic.

Q: What's green and yellow and eats nuts?
A: Gonorrhea.

Q: What's red and slimy and crawls up a woman's leg?
A: A homesick abortion.

Q: What do you call an anorexic with a yeast infection?
A: Quarter-pounder with cheese.

Q: What's funnier than a dead baby?
A: A dead baby in a clown costume.

Q: What's funnier than a dead baby?
A: A dead baby sitting next to a kid with Down syndrome.

Q: What's funnier that a drunk clown?
A: A drunk clown with Down syndrome.

Q: How do you know when a baby is a dead baby?
A: The dog plays with it more.

Q: What present do you get for a dead baby?
A: A dead puppy.

Q: How do you make a dead baby float?
A: Take your foot off its head.

Q: How do you make a dead baby float?
A: One scoop of ice cream and two scoops of dead baby.

Q: What do you get when you cut a dead baby with a razor?
A: An erection.

Q: How do you stop a baby crawling around in circles?
A: Nail its other hand to the floor.

Q: What's worse than ten dead babies nailed to one tree?
A: One dead baby nailed to ten trees.

Q: How do you fit fifty babies into a bucket?
A: With a blender.

Q: How do you get them out again?
A: Doritos.

Q: What's blue and bloated and floating in your beer?
A: A dead baby with fetal alcohol syndrome.

Q: What's brown and taps on the window?
A: A baby in a microwave.

Q: What's brown and gurgles?
A: A baby in a casserole.

Q: What's black and red and sizzles?
A: A dead baby on a barbecue.

Q: What goes *plop, plop, fizz, fizz*?
A: Twin dead babies in an acid bath.

Q: What gets louder as it gets smaller?
A: A dead baby in a trash compactor.

Q: How do you stop a baby from falling down a manhole?
A: Stick a spear through its head.

Q: What's white and red and hangs from a telephone wire?
A: A baby shot through a snow blower.

Q: What's red and is found in all four corners of a room?
A: A dead baby who's been playing with a chain saw.

Q: What's cold, blue, and doesn't move?
A: A dead baby in your freezer.

Q: What's pink, flies, and squeals?
A: A baby fired from a catapult.

Q: What do you call the baby when it lands?
A: Free pizza.

Q: What's the best thing about a Siamese twin baby?
A: Threesomes.

Q: What bounces up and down at sixty miles per hour?
A: A dead baby tied to the back of a truck.

Q: Why do you put a dead baby feet-first into a blender?
A: So you can come on its face.

Q: What's the difference between a rock and a dead baby?
A: You can't fuck a rock.

Q: What's the difference between a banana and a dead baby?
A: You don't come all over a banana before eating it.

Q: What's more fun than nailing a dead baby to a wall?
A: Ripping it off again.

Q: What's more fun than throwing a dead baby off the cliff?
A: Catching it with a pitchfork.

Q: What's more fun than swinging dead babies around on a clothesline?
A: Stopping them with a shovel.

A man gets a phone call from the hospital. His wife has been in an accident. The man rushes to the emergency room where he's met by the doctor. They sit down in the waiting room and the doctor, with a very solemn look on his face, starts to speak.

"I have some bad news," the doctor says.

"Doc, don't tell me my wife's dead. I just can't take it. Really, I can't take it. I love her."

"We did all we could," the doctor continues.

"Doc, just tell me, did she make it?"

"As I was saying, we did all we could. Right now she's in a vegetative state, which is likely where she'll remain for the rest of her life. She can stay here overnight, but after that, you'll have to take her home because your insurance doesn't cover this type of thing."

The man slumps over in his chair.

The doctor continues, "With the right care, which will include you feeding her six times a day, cleaning her, and giving her constant care on a daily basis, she'll likely live for at least another twenty-five years."

The man slumps lower in his chair and starts to cry.

"As I mentioned," the doctor says, "your insurance doesn't cover this kind of care, so you'll have to purchase your wife's medical equipment, which will cost you around fifty thousand dollars."

At this news, the man starts to cry uncontrollably.

The doctor reaches over, puts his hand on the man's shoulder, and says, "Hey, look at me." The guy looks up, and the doctor smiles and says, "I'm just fucking with you; she's dead."